MY THOUGHTS

FOUR ESSAYS

DALE D. CANNADY

authorHOUSE®

AuthorHouse™
1663 Liberty Drive
Bloomington, IN 47403
www.authorhouse.com
Phone: 1-800-839-8640

Published by AuthorHouse 4/09/2012

ISBN: 978-1-4685-5990-3 (sc)
ISBN: 978-1-4685-5989-7 (hc)
ISBN: 978-1-4685-5988-0 (e)

Library of Congress Control Number: 2012904368

FOREWORD

The four essays herein are entitled:

1. A Permanent Calendar
2. Toward More Precise Written Language
3. Settlements and Boundaries
4. The Possibility of Cycles

The essays are the result of considerable thought over a long part of my life. Long term interest in world events and in books deemed interesting to me contributed to the views expressed in the essays. Hopefully, the essays will arouse curiosity and the interest of others concerning some of the ideas set out in the essays.

The essays are not accompanied by a list of references, but three sources of information should be cited:

1. *Encyclopedia Britannica*
2. *The Presidencies*, Editor Michael Nelson, published 1996 by Salamander Books Ltd., London
3. *Presidential Campaigns*, Paul Boller Jr., published 1984 and 1985 by Oxford University Press.

Geography and history have been fascinating subjects to me as far back as my elementary school years. A belated entrance into college with intent to major in economics and business, followed by brief consideration of a major in foreign relations, ended with a Bachelor of Arts in Geography. The full range of courses in geography was accompanied by courses in economic geology, geomorphology, weather and climate, oceanography, physical and social anthropology, history, and political science. Interest in these areas has continued throughout my life.

Some training in cartography and a most fortunate social contact led to a career in city planning in Seattle, Washington and Portland, Oregon. Some of the comments in one of the essays reflect that experience.

Comments from my wife Mitzi and our daughter Lila have been helpful as the essays were completed. Mitzi's typing and Lila's efforts have been essential to publication of the essays and are deeply appreciated.

DDC

A PERMANENT ANNUAL CALENDAR

AN ESSAY
BY DALE D. CANNADY

Over time, proposals have been made to improve upon the Gregorian solar calendar, now in use throughout the world for civic purposes, by dividing the calendar year into a different arrangement of days, weeks, and months. This is because the days of the year fall on different dates, owing to the odd number of days in the 365-day calendar year. Further compounding the difficulty with the Gregorian solar calendar is the insertion of a February 29 Leap Year Day at certain four-year intervals. Proposals to change the solar calendar have met with resistance, probably due to the complexity of those proposals.

A permanent solar calendar, however, can be made with a simple change in the Gregorian solar calendar: adopting a 364-day year, with the inclusion of an unnumbered Year End Day, and an unnumbered Leap Year Day at certain four-year intervals.

THE GREGORIAN SOLAR CALENDAR

Pope Gregory XIII promulgated the Gregorian solar calendar in March 1582, to correct an error in the length of the year in the Julian solar calendar. The Julian calendar, adopted in 45 BC at the direction of the Roman dictator Julius Caesar, estimated the length of the year at 365.25 days. The actual length is nearly 365.2422 days.

The Gregorian solar calendar's response to the odd number of days in the year is the addition of a 29th date (Leap Year Day) at the end of February at most four-year intervals. Further adjustment of the four year intervals must be made at certain 400 year intervals, because century years not divisible by 400 are not given a February 29 Leap Year Day.

That still does not solve the problem. Astronomers have determined that after 2000 years, a much longer period of time, another adjustment in the addition of the Leap Year Day will be needed. Even that change will not bring absolute accuracy to the solar calendar.

OBSTACLES TO CREATING A PERMANENT CALENDAR

The major obstacle to creating a permanent calendar is that the solar year is just under 365 ¼ days long, instead of an even number of days. If the year had an even number of days, each day could bear the same date every year.

Another problem is humankind's use of a seven-day week since ancient times. The solar year contains one day and ¼ more than 52 seven-day weeks. In addition, those weeks are divided into the traditional 12 months of the solar year.

The Gregorian solar calendar varies the length of those months somewhat, because the four seasons of the year are not exactly equal in length. The elliptical orbit of the Earth around the Sun, and the timing of the December and June solstices and the March and September equinoxes, determine the lengths of the four seasons.

SIMPLE STEPS TO CREATE A
PERMANENT ANNUAL CALENDAR

The addition of Leap Year Days must continue to be made at intervals, determined by astronomers as being necessary, to keep the calendar synchronized with the Earth's annual orbit around the Sun. A permanent annual calendar can be created, however, provided these two steps are taken:

1. Replace the February 29 date -- now used in Leap Years -- with a Leap Year Day when needed at the end of February, giving that Leap Year Day neither a number date nor a weekday name.
2. Replace the last date of the year -- currently December 31 -- with a day called Year End Day, giving that Year End Day neither a number date nor a week-day name.

A permanent annual calendar cannot be created if a Leap Year Day or a Year End Day is given a number date or one of the seven weekday names.

The following page shows a permanent annual calendar. It contains the present twelve months, 52 seven-day weeks, and a total of 364 days plus a Year End Day. The calendar also shows where a Leap Year Day can be observed at appropriate intervals of time, as determined by astronomers.

THE PERMANENT ANNUAL CALENDAR

JANUARY

						1
2	3	4	5	6	7	8
9	10	11	12	13	14	15
16	17	18	19	20	21	22
23	24	25	26	27	28	29
30	31					

FEBRUARY

		1	2	3	4	5
6	7	8	9	10	11	12
13	14	15	16	17	18	19
20	21	22	23	24	25	26
27	28	LYD				

MARCH

		1	2	3	4	5
6	7	8	9	10	11	12
13	14	15	16	17	18	19
20	21	22	23	24	25	26
27	28	29	30	31		

APRIL

					1	2
3	4	5	6	7	8	9
10	11	12	13	14	15	16
17	18	19	20	21	22	23
24	25	26	27	28	29	30

MAY

1	2	3	4	5	6	7
8	9	10	11	12	13	14
15	16	17	18	19	20	21
22	23	24	25	26	27	28
29	30	31				

JUNE

		1	2	3	4	
5	6	7	8	9	10	11
12	13	14	15	16	17	18
19	20	21	22	23	24	25
26	27	28	29	30		

JULY

					1	2
3	4	5	6	7	8	9
10	11	12	13	14	15	16
17	18	19	20	21	22	23
24	25	26	27	28	29	30
31						

AUGUST

	1	2	3	4	5	6
7	8	9	10	11	12	13
14	15	16	17	18	19	20
21	22	23	24	25	26	27
28	29	30	31			

SEPTEMBER

					1	2	3
4	5	6	7	8	9	10
11	12	13	14	15	16	17
18	19	20	21	22	23	24
25	26	27	28	29	30	

OCTOBER

						1
2	3	4	5	6	7	8
9	10	11	12	13	14	15
16	17	18	19	20	21	22
23	24	25	26	27	28	29
30	31					

NOVEMBER

		1	2	3	4	5
6	7	8	9	10	11	12
13	14	15	16	17	18	19
20	21	22	23	24	25	26
27	28	29	30			

DECEMBER

					1	2	3
4	5	6	7	8	9	10
11	12	13	14	15	16	17
18	19	20	21	22	23	24
25	26	27	28	29	30	YED

LYD - a Leap Year Day, neither numbered nor bearing a weekday name, would be used at the end of February almost every fourth year as determined by astronomers.

YED - a Year End Day, neither numbered nor bearing a weekday name, would replace the December 31 now used on annual calendars.

3

Regarding the listing of months and numerical dates on the permanent annual calendar, it will be noted at once that no names have been used for the seven days of each week. This leaves an essential third step to be taken, and that is to decide how the seven weekday names should be placed on the numerical dates listed on this proposed permanent calendar.

MAKING THE DECISION

Making the decision on placing the seven weekday names on the proposed permanent calendar is an appropriate task for the United Nations, because all nations using the Gregorian solar calendar have historic dates and holidays that are important to them. Therefore, it would be necessary to compromise in determining where the seven names of weekdays would be placed on the permanent calendar. Agreement on which of the seven days in the week would be assigned the January 1 date is essential. The choice made for that day would set the pattern for the entire 364 numbered days and 52 weeks of the year. With that selection made, the pattern would be set for all ensuing years.

A RECOMMENDATION FROM A UNITED STATES PERSPECTIVE

This recommendation for weekday names for the numerical dates would place January 1 on Saturday, immediately following Year End Day, and would result in American holidays as follows:

Jan. 1	Saturday	New Year's Day
Jan. 16	Sunday	Martin Luther King Jr. Day
Feb. 21	Monday	U. S. A. Presidents Day
May 1	Sunday	May Day (an important day for many other nations)
May 30	Monday	U. S. A. Memorial Day (originally set following the American Civil War)
July 4	Monday	U. S. A. Independence Day
Sept. 5	Monday	U. S. A. Labor Day
Nov. 11	Friday	U. S. A. Veterans Day (World War I ended on Friday, November 11, 1918)

Nov. 24	Thursday	U. S. A. Thanksgiving Day (the fourth Thursday of November)
Dec. 23	Friday	a Muslim worship day
Dec. 24	Saturday	a Jewish worship day
Dec. 25	Sunday	a Christian worship day

This recommendation for weekday names applied to these particular dates would be advantageous for both management and labor in the United States. It would provide an appropriate holiday structure from the workers' standpoint and, simultaneously, make possible precise management scheduling of operational closures in production and service fields. Under this recommendation, Year End Day would not divide a workweek into two parts, because it would follow a Friday (December 30) and precede Saturday (January 1, New Year's Day).

One problem for management and workers to resolve would be that Leap Year Day would follow a Monday (February 28) and precede a Tuesday (March 1), thus periodically adding a sixth workday to that week. However, this difficulty, which would occur only at four-year intervals, could be resolved within contract negotiations.

This schedule of holidays would also work well for United States school teachers, for their students, and for the parents of students who plan their vacations around their children's school schedules. Only Thanksgiving (traditionally a four-day United States school holiday) would significantly interrupt weekly school instruction. All other recommended school holiday dates would occur on weekend days, or at the beginning or end of the school week. Mid-week holidays would no longer interrupt the flow of educational instruction, as they do now.

GENERAL ADVANTAGES

Regardless of the weekday name selected for January 1, the permanent annual calendar would have these advantages. There would be no annual changes in the dates of the seven days of the week. Week lengths and month names would remain unchanged. The lengths of ten of the months would remain unchanged, but February would always have 28 days, and December would always have 30 days. Events occurring on Year End Day (YED) or Leap Year Day (LYD) would be noted as having occurred on those particular days of a year, but not on a number date or a weekday name.

Another important advantage, which would help to facilitate adoption of this annual calendar, would be that no one on Earth would feel that he/she had lost the anniversary of his/her birth, or of any other significant past-personal or historical date.

The great advantage would be, of course, that the annual calendar would be permanent, and a new calendar would not be needed every year, as is the present situation.

INITIATING USE

The permanent annual calendar could not be put into use until agreement was reached on the weekday name for January 1 (and thus for the other 363 numerical dates of the calendar year). Year End Day would follow the 364 dated days, resulting in a 365-day calendar year. Then it would be necessary to await the appropriate year to initiate the permanent annual calendar. That time would arrive under our present annual calendar usage when December 31 (to be changed to Year End Day) occurred on a weekday name immediately preceding the weekday name selected for January 1 as the beginning of the permanent annual calendar. Like Year End Day, Leap Year Day would not be a numbered calendar day.

REGARDING LUNAR CALENDARS

The Moon has held significance for humans since ancient times. As it orbits the Earth, our Moon does have an impact on Earth. It creates the tides in the oceans, and even creates minor tidal movements in the Earth's crust. It may have some minor influence over ever-changing weather conditions. In its orbits around Earth, it reflects the Sun's light into Earth's nights.

However, the Moon's influence on the Earth is negligible, when compared with that of the Sun:

1. The Sun's gravity holds the Earth in orbit around the Sun.
2. The Sun provides heat and light to the Earth.

3. The annual orbit of the Earth around the Sun sets the length of the year.
4. The 23.5-degree tilt of the Earth, in its annual elliptical orbit around the Sun, determines the four seasons.
5. The Earth's daily revolution during its annual orbit around the Sun, in addition to its 23.5-degree tilt, determines the varying length of Earth's days and nights.

Today's scientific knowledge about the Sun and Moon suggest that reliance on a permanent annual solar calendar would be more advantageous than reliance upon lunar calculations for a lunar calendar. Although some religious groups use either a lunar calendar or lunar calculations to set the dates of their celebrations, fasts, feasts, and holy days, a permanent annual solar calendar would make it possible to establish consistent dates for those events. For example, Christian groups could agree to set Easter on either the second or the third Sunday of April, rather than having the date of Easter change from year to year, as it does now with lunar calculations. Other religious groups could as easily establish consistent dates for their religious events on this permanent annual solar calendar.

DDC

TOWARD MORE PRECISE
WRITTEN LANGUAGE

AN ESSAY
BY DALE D. CANNADY

Speech (oral language) must have developed gradually within small groups as humans migrated from region to region, until they occupied most of the Earth. Subsequent conversion of some oral languages into written language is one of the most important technical advances made by humans. It has allowed shared communication and learning among much larger groups of people, and has made possible ever increasing advancements of science and technology.

As humans have increased in numbers and gathered into wider groupings, many lesser-used languages and dialects have disappeared entirely or been subsumed within more dominant languages. Simultaneously, progress in refinement and simplification of more widely used languages has occurred, through both evolution in everyday speech and the efforts of linguists to develop and improve symbols that represent the sounds in spoken words. Elimination of superfluous sounds and symbols has helped to simplify words and names, and to create written languages that more precisely indicate the actual pronunciation of words and names.

Unfortunately, the world's languages still maintain traditional spellings that no longer match modern-day pronunciations. This makes learning a second or third language a daunting task, even when alphabets remain relatively consistent, as they do in Western Europe, the Americas, and former colonial possessions of Western European empires. Meeting new words and decoding their precise pronunciations is difficult, especially for English speakers, because that language is less phonetically based than most.

If linguists were to simplify and universalize the symbols used to denote specific sounds, the learning of new languages (especially Western European languages) would become much easier. The purpose of this essay is to present a system of precise symbols for sounds in the English language that would make possible more precise spelling and pronunciation of words and names by all users of the language -- and all those seeking to learn the language.

HISTORICAL CONTEXT

Progress in the development of symbols for pronunciation and spelling in the Western areas of the world began with the Phoenicians and empires of the Middle East. Further advances came in ancient Greece, the Roman Empire, and then in the various languages of Europe. However, progress in the development of symbols for sounds, and the means of translating words and names into written language, came about in much different ways in lands far removed from the Western areas of the world. Those methods are apparent in the writing and printing of languages in the Middle East and the Far East.

Until recent times, the isolation by distance of the different language groups meant that few people learned a language other than their native tongue. Far fewer learned one of the much different languages developed around varying alphabet structures. Now, due to increasingly rapid transportation and communication, a more closely-knit world has come into existence, and contacts between different language groups are multiplying throughout the world. The goal for language experts in all the language areas of the world ought to be the development of a concise set of symbols, to represent the sounds in words and speech within the major languages. This would make languages more precisely spelled and more accurately spoken; it would make languages more easily learned and more easily and accurately translated into other languages. This could help greatly to minimize misunderstandings and conflicts between the different groups of people and nations throughout the world.

THE ENGLISH LANGUAGE

The English language is only one of the written languages of the Western world, but it has become one of the major languages of the world. It was planted in many areas of the world during the era of British Empire dominance, and its use as a communication medium has been increasing since World War II. The English language has proven valuable because it is both an innovator of words and a borrower of words from other languages. However, these strengths have allowed English to drift from its original more phonetic course, making it more difficult to speak and spell, even for native speakers. Making it easier to learn English is highly important, not only for the native-born in English-speaking areas and for non-English-speaking immigrants into those areas, but also for all peoples wishing to use the English language as a world-wide communication medium.

Needed for the English language is a system of symbols for concise phonetic pronunciations of the sounds in the language. Presented herein is such a system of symbols to facilitate precision in the spelling and pronunciation of words and names. In presenting this system, it should be noted at the outset that the full value of a system of symbols for concise phonetic pronunciation can only be gained through follow-up use of the system for both precise spelling and phonetic pronunciation of words and names.

THE PRESENT SOUNDS OF LETTERS IN ENGLISH

The present system of symbols for sounds in the English language is the English alphabet, which contains 26 letters (or symbols) representing 21 consonants and 5 vowels. Some of the 21 letters (or symbols) representing consonants are given more than one sound in English speech. This means that the English alphabet does not depict all the sounds in ordinary English language speech. Linguists have determined that the English language uses 43 sounds consisting of single alphabet sounds or blends of alphabet sounds. The 43 sounds can be divided into groups as follows; 18 consonant sounds, 9 consonant blends, and 16 vowel sounds.

Each of the 5 vowel symbols has been given one or more related vowel pronunciations. The English language also contains a unique vowel sound bearing the OO symbol; that unique vowel sound can for phonetic purposes be labeled a medium length U vowel sound. It needs an alphabetic symbol to differentiate it from another double OO symbol now in use.

Five of the total 16 vowel sounds are represented by these combinations AI, OI, AU, EU, and OU. In the interest of phonetics, continued use of these 5 combinations is desirable.

The current variety of pronunciations presents phonetic confusion for both English learners and spellers.

RECOMMENDED SOUND/SYMBOL PRONUNCIATIONS

The following is a proposed system for concise phonetic pronunciations that could be used for more precise spelling of words and names in the English language.

The 18 English consonant sounds are represented by the symbols B, P, D, T, V, F, W, H, J, Y, G, K, R, L, M, N, S, and Z. The 9 English consonant blends are shown herein as C (TS), CH (TSH), X (KS), voiced TH, NG, ZH, non-voiced TH, SH, and HW. Instead of the present English alphabet recitation (A, B, C, etc.), each of the 18 consonants and the HW consonant blend could be verbally recited with a long EI vowel sound (as described later) following each of them. The C (TS), CH (TSH), X (KS), voiced TH, NG, ZH, non-voiced TH, and SH could be verbally recited with a short E vowel sound preceding each of them.

In this essay, for phonetic purposes, each of the 5 vowel symbols has been given the label of either a long vowel sound or a short vowel sound as demonstrated below.

LONG VOWELS		SHORT VOWELS	
A	(or AA) as in water	A	as in bat
E	(or EI) as in rein	E	as in set
I	(or IE) as in lien	I	as in bit
O	(or OE) as in fold	O	as in lot
U	(or UE) as in duty	U	as in but

The 5 vowel symbols (A, E, I, O, and U) may be given either a long vowel sound or a short vowel sound, depending on "sound convenience" (a choice in favor of the easiest pronunciation) within the words in which they are used. For clarity and ease of pronunciation, the five long vowel sounds would be used in vowel recitation. For the medium length U vowel sound, cited earlier, a new Ø symbol could be used.

CONSONANT SOUNDS AND CONSONANT BLENDS

The following chart portrays 27 of the 43 sounds in English identified by linguists; these are the 18 consonant sounds and the 9 consonant blends. The placement in the chart of those consonant sounds and consonant blends is made so that similarities and differences in their pronunciations will be more evident.

CONSONANTS		CONSONANT BLENDS		
Voiced	**Non-Voiced**	**Non-Voiced**	**Voiced**	**Non-Voiced**
B	P			
D	T	C(TS)		CH(TSH)
			TH	TH
V	F			
W	H			HW
Y				
J				
G	K(Q)	X(KS)		
R				
L				
M				
N			NG	
Z	S		ZH	SH

The 12 consonant sounds in the first column on the left are sounded (voiced) and the 6 in the second column are breathed (non-voiced). The three consonant blends in the fourth column from the left are voiced, while those in the third and fifth columns are non-voiced.

For the non-English speaker learning English, there will be confusion unless the difference between voiced and non-voiced is explained by example. Careful pronunciation of each consonant and each consonant blend is essential for accurate spelling and reading.

THE CONSONANTS

The following is both a description of the consonants in the English language, and also a way of simplifying and teaching phonetic pronunciation of those consonants.

The consonants B, P, V, and F in the first and second columns in the above chart are formed with the lips, with B and V being voiced sounds, and P and F being non-voiced sounds. (For concise phonetics, the present inconsistent use of PH and GH for the F sound in such words as *philosophy* and *laugh* would be discontinued.)

The D and T sounds are made with the tip of the tongue at the roof of the mouth. The D is the voiced sound, and T the non-voiced sound. (The present confusing pronunciation of T as an SH sound in words such as *solution* could be met by changing the spelling to *solusiun.)*

Both W and Y are voiced consonants. In the English language both W and Y are now also used in the spelling of some vowel sounds, for example: *boy, cow, law, ay(yes)*. This is acceptable, but where either the W or Y is a separate consonant sound, beginning another syllable as in *a-ware* or *O-wen,* a hyphen (-) is required for accurate pronunciation. This must be carefully explained to a non-English speaker learning English.

The non-voiced H in the second column of the chart is a distinct consonant sound, when used at the beginning of a word or syllable; the other use of H is the non-voiced second part in the consonant blends, shown in the fourth and fifth columns of the chart. Where the H sound follows another consonant sound, and is not part of a consonant blend (as in the voiced TH, the non-voiced TH, the ZH, and SH), it would be preceded by a hyphen (-). This would show that it is merely indicative of a non-voiced sound, as in the German province name *T-huringia,* the *T-har* desert in India, the Arabic boat *d-hou,* the Mongol *K-han* and the word *g-host.* To clarify and emphasize concise phonetic pronunciation, the non-voiced H in such English words as *g-host and g-hastly,* the H would be eliminated. In time, use of the hyphen and the H in the foreign titles, names, and words could be eliminated in order to emphasize concise phonetic pronunciation of the consonant preceding the non-voiced H.

The letter J is a voiced sound. The J might be confused with either a DY consonant blend sound resembling such blends as the BY blend (as in *Bjorn Borg,* the tennis player) and the FY blend (as in the word *fjord* in the Scandinavian languages). The English language J is not a DY; it is a distinct voiced consonant sound.

At present, the last J sound in some English words is represented by DG, as in these words: *badge, lodge, ledge, ridge, judge.* For concise phonetics, this confusing use of DG would be discontinued and replaced with J; the result would be *baj, loj, lej, rij,* and *juj.* (It might be helpful to cease placing a dot over the lower case j, because of its visual similarity to the lower case i).

Also, the G is now given the J sound in many English words or names, such as *gist, gesture, Geraldine,* and *George.* Under this proposal, this unnecessary and inconsistent J pronunciation of G would be discontinued.

The G and K sounds are the voiced and non-voiced sounds, as in the words *garb* and *kit.* Under this plan the K would be used for the K sound only. Use of the C for the K sound would be eliminated, to end the present confusion between the use of K, as in the word *kit,* and the use of C, as in the word *cat.* The use of K is preferable, because it leaves the C for use as the (TS) blend and CH for the (TSH) blend. (Also, for concise phonetics the use of CK for the K sound as in *lick* or *back* would be discontinued. Use of the CH for the K sound as in *choral* or *chord* would be eliminated too.)

In the German language, the deep throated K sound in the word *achtung* differs somewhat from the K sound in the city name *Kiel.* In the English language, the K sound in the words *accord* or *occupied* is somewhat different from the K sound in the words *beckon, lack,* or *king.* The difference is due to the location of the K sound inside the mouth, and that is determined by the relationship of the K sound to the vowel sound preceding or following it. Therefore, to avoid phonetic confusion there should be only one K consonant sound in English.

The letters K and (Q) in the English alphabet represent only one sound, rather than two, creating confusion for English language learners. Possible continued use of the (Q) alternative will be discussed later under Vowel Sounds.

The letters R and L might be labeled the "tongue twisters" of language.

Scottish people "roll" the R a bit when pronouncing it. Some natives of Japan have difficulty pronouncing the L sound. These two consonants do seem to be the most difficult to pronounce. (The H after R as in *rheumatoid* should be eliminated and the EU changed to U or UE.)

Among consonants, the R and L are especially interesting because of their impact on the pronunciation of vowels preceding them. The vowels A, E, I, O, and U receive a clear short vowel pronunciation before L, as in *Al, el, ill, Ollie,* and *ultra.* The vowels E and I receive a clear short vowel pronunciation before R as in *errant* and *irregular,* but do not in *sterling* and *bird.* O and U also receive one that is not clear in *cord* and *curb.*

The vowel A receives a clear long vowel pronunciation before R, as in *art,* and in some instances receives a clear long A before L, as in the pronunciation of the word *qualm.* Where necessary, a long vowel pronunciation of the vowels A, E, I, O, and U before either R or L could best be assured by the use of an alternative long vowel combination. (See the later discussion of AA, EI, IE, OE, and UE.)

Spanish speakers have pronounced LL as Y in the words *llano* and *llama.* Some time ago a news report, regarding a conference on the Spanish language, stated that there was agreement that one L could be eliminated from this spelling. With L being used in other words and names in the Spanish language, such as *lariat* and *Las Vegas,* the pronunciation of *lano* and *lama,* could begin with the L sound, rather than a Y sound.

The letters M and N could be called the "hummers" of the English language. The M is a voiced lip sound, and the N is a voiced tongue sound.

The Z and S sounds are voiced and non-voiced sounds, respectively. For concise phonetics, the PS in *psycho* would be eliminated, and the spelling changed to *saiko.* (Reasons for the ai will be shown later under The 21 Combinations.)

In English, the S is also used to signify the plural of nouns. When the S follows P, T, F, K, and the non-voiced TH, it remains an S sound. However, when the S follows B, D, the voiced TH, V, G, R, L, M, N, and NG, through "speech convenience" it automatically becomes a Z sound.

In English the ES is used to signify the plural of words ending in CH (TSH), J, X, Z, S, ZH, and SH. Here through "speech convenience" the ES automatically becomes an EZ sound.

These oral conversions of the S to a Z sound in some words, present a problem for English learners. Therefore, where the sound in speech is actually Z instead of S, there is need to point this out to the learners.

THE CONSONANT BLENDS

The C (TS) in the third column, and the CH (TSH) in the chart's fifth column, are non-voiced consonant blends. The C (TS) is phonetically used in such words as *convince and presence*. (The "silent" or unpronounced E at the end of these words should be eliminated). Some of the Slavic languages use C for the (TS) sound and the CH for a (TSH) sound. The Italian language uses CC, as in the word *bocci*. Phonetically under this proposed system, it would be spelled *bochi*.

The X consonant blend in the chart's third column is followed by (KS). Uses here are the X as a letter in the word *hexagon,* and the KS as the plural of words ending in K. The letter X is necessary to differentiate it from the plural KS.

The TH in the chart's fourth column is a voiced consonant blend, while the TH in the fifth column is a non-voiced consonant blend. There appears to be no good reason for the TH to be either voiced or non-voiced. Apparently, the distinction is simply "sound convenience"; this distinction must be explained to English language learners.

The NG consonant blend in the chart's fourth column represents the NG sound in such words as *swimming, kicking, slang, thing,* or *gong,* in which the NG is left in a "hanging" position at the end of words. Where NG appears to be more strongly voiced, as in *bingo, angry,* and *hungry,* a saving of an additional letter symbol (G) appears to be the purpose. More precise spelling would be *bing-go, ang-gry,* and *hung-gry.* This NG consonant blend is different from such consonant combinations as ND or NT, because the G is emphasized less in *ring* than the D or T in *bend* or *hunt.*

The ZH and SH consonant blends, in the chart's fourth and fifth columns, utilize the Z and S with the H. The ZH is the voiced blend, and the SH is the non-voiced blend, and would be spelled accordingly.

English makes use of the letters WH in such words as *why* and *when.* It is difficult to understand why this odd usage persists, since it creates spelling problems for English children. The original sound in *why* and *when* actually is the HW consonant blend, as shown in the fifth column of the chart. More precise use of the W is shown in other combinations, such as *dwarf, twain, swain,* and *Gwendolyn.*

CONCLUSIONS REGARDING CONSONANTS
AND CONSONANT BLENDS

The 18 consonants and 9 consonant blends in the English language are the building blocks of that language. Precision in their identification, phonetic pronunciation, and use in speech and in the spelling of words would assist both native-born and non-English speakers learning English.

Further examination of the 18 consonants and 9 consonant blends reveals the extent of their possible use; they may be followed by another consonant at the beginning of words or syllables.

The B, P, D, T, G, and K consonants are easily combined with an R consonant following them. The S and Z can be combined with L, T, or W. The M or N "hummers" can be combined with a Y consonant following either of them. (The GN in *filet mignon,* borrowed from the French language, is properly pronounced *mi-nyon*).

The F can easily combine with an R or L consonant following it. Other common consonant combinations include *slam, blend, trap, frank, fling, twin, grip,* and *drink.* Many more combinations are possible.

Other languages reveal the possibility of more combinations. Examples are the Scandinavian *fjord (fyord),* the *Tlingit* Indians, the Russian name *Vladimir,* the Korean automobile *Hyundai,* and the Slavic name *Hruska.* However, such combinations as the Russian river *Dnieper,* the city *Tver,* and the African *gnu* reveal a swift omission of an intervening vowel.

Among consonant blends, the SH or ZH can be combined with an R, L, or W following either one. The voiced TH seems much less likely to be combined with an R or L consonant following it, than does the non-voiced TH. The HW, NG, X (KS), and CH (TSH) do not combine with another consonant following them. The C (TS) might be combined with an L consonant.

It is important to note that doubling of a consonant following a vowel is a means not only of ensuring accurate pronunciation of the five short vowel sounds, but also of clarifying the spellings and meanings of words. For example: *liter, litter, lager, lagging, sober, sobbing.* However, a consonant should not be doubled if long vowel pronunciation of the preceding vowel is desired.

EXISTING VOWEL SOUNDS

Effort to advance concise spelling and use of the 18 consonant sounds and 9 consonant blend sounds in the English language, as discussed above, is easy compared to seeking improved symbolic identification of vowel sounds.

Great variety and inconsistency exist in present vowel usage and spelling in the English language, as it has developed over time. At present there are diverse word spellings which are survivors from Old English. The "silent" or unpronounced E after a consonant preceded by a vowel, as in the words *hale, cede, fine, tune,* and *cone* was pronounced in Old English. (In most instances, the obvious solution to this problem is to remove the E from the end of the word, and alter the vowel spelling preceding the consonant.) Some other word spellings came with the Norman (French) conquest of England in the 11th century. Clearly there is need for a more precise array of vowel sound symbols.

The English alphabet letters A, E, I, O, U have come down through the Latin alphabet from the Greek letters *Alpha, Eta, Iota, Omega,* and *Upsilon.* The only guidance those offer in determining desirable vowel pronunciation and spelling is that *Alpha* begins with a short A sound and the other four begin with long vowel sounds.

The English language now has six long vowel sounds as shown in these words:

1. *hart, ark, harm, father, arbor, calm.*
2. *hay, hey, hate, rain, rein, reign, bay.*
3. *heed, seen, scene, bean, lead, lien, siege, ski.*
4. *high, find, fine, eye, pint, bye, aye, aisle, height, ait.*
5. *home, own, foe, go, loan, beau, low, though.*
6. *hoot, loose, boot, lose, lieu, deuce, fruit, sue, newt, through.*

English has five short vowel sounds as used in these words:

1. *bat, band, lack, tank, fact, ban, draught, draft.*
2. *bet, bent, mesh, lend, rent, net, any.*
3. *bit, fix, hick, mint, flint, drink.*
4. *hot, fond, lot, bottle, cot, mottle.*
5. *but, fudge, nut, fund, hut, tough.*

As noted earlier, in some English language words such as *put, foot,* and *root,* a medium length U sound exists. At present there is no English vowel symbol for this sound, but it sounds akin to one of the German language umlaut sounds.

In the German language there are 3 umlaut vowel sounds: Ä, Ü, and Ö -- all specially marked to distinguish them from A, U, and O. The Ä umlaut sounds like the short English A vowel sound described above. Any English speaking person who has attempted to speak German will remember the difficulty in trying to properly pucker the lips to pronounce the Ö umlaut.

The German (Ü) umlaut sounds similar to the medium length U sound in English words, such as *put, foot,* and *root,* but the umlaut symbol used in German could be confused with a double ii in English print. Therefore, a special symbol for the English medium length U vowel sound is needed; a Ø is proposed.

The English language also has four other vowel sounds, shown as vowel combinations in these names and words:

1. *Hoyle, coy, coin, boy, loin.*
2. *Hawkins, haul, awl, caught, fall, ought, off.*
3. *Hugh, cute, you, few, beauty, hue, use, view.*
4. *Houk, count, lounge, cow, out.*

OBSTACLES TO PHONETIC PRONUNCIATION AND PRECISE SPELLING

Examination of vowel usage in the English language reveals a number of obstacles to concise pronunciation and precise spelling. English now has:

I. These different spellings providing two long A vowel sounds:

1. As in *farm, calm, father, wander, about, akin, asea, await.*
2. As in *late, Gael, fail, rain.*
3. As in *vein, Leif, rein, seine.*

II. These different spellings providing a long E vowel sound;

    1. As in *lead, bean.*
    2. As in *seen, scene, mete.*
    3. As in *lien, siege.*

III. These different spellings providing a long I vowel sound:

    1. As in *fine, find, pint, lie, dial.*
    2. As in *high, height.*
    3. As in *isle, ait, aye, aisle, bayou.*
    4. As in *eye, buy, bye.*

IV. These different spellings providing a long O vowel sound:

    1. As in *loaf, cone, bow, phone.*
    2. As in *though.*
    3. As in *beau.*

V. These different spellings that are expected to produce a long U vowel sound:

    1. As in *sue, true.*
    2. As in *booth, lose, loose, boot.*
    3. As in *stew, newt, through.*

VI. These different spellings given the medium length U vowel sound (the German umlaut Ü).

    1. As in *foot, soot.*
    2. As in *pull, full.*

VII. These different spellings given a short A vowel sound:

    1. As in *bat, draft.*
    2. As in *draught, laugh.*

VIII. These different spellings given a short E vowel sound:

    1. As in *bent, trend.*
    2. As in *any.*

IX. These inconsistent and confusing pronunciations for a short I vowel sound and a long I vowel sound in similarly spelled words:

    1. As in *mint, hint* (short i).
    2. As in *pint, kind* (long i).

X. These different spellings given a short O vowel sound (which sounds like the first of the long A sounds listed above):

    1. As in *cot, bottle, mop.* (It should be noted here that in such words as *love, of,* and *covenant,* the O is mistakenly given the more "sound convenient" short U vowel sound rather than a short O vowel sound. A change in spelling would help here.)

XI. These different spellings given a short U vowel sound:

    1. As in *fun, fudge, nut.*
    2. As in *tough, bluff.*

XII. These different spellings of four other vowel sounds:

    1. As in *coy, coin.*
    2. As in *haul, hall, aught, awl, off.*
    3. As in *cute, you, few, feud, use, beauty, view.*
    4. As in *count, cow.*

DEVELOPING RECOMMENDATIONS FOR VOWEL SOUNDS

At this point, it is evident that significant choices must be made, to assure specific long vowel phonetic pronunciation of the letters A, E, and I. In present English language, the letter A now has two long vowel pronunciations as in *father* and *gate*. The letter E in *rein* is now given a long A vowel pronunciation. Both the letters E and I are now given a long E vowel pronunciation as in *bean* and *lien*. When either E or A are combined with Y (as in e*ye* or *aye*) the Y pronunciation, used now, sounds like the present long I pronunciation in *find* or *dial*.

In developing recommendations for vowel sounds and concise pronunciation, three issues are apparent. The first is recognition of the "fluidity in sound" when speech is gliding from the pronunciation of a long vowel sound to pronunciation of another long vowel sound, or to some short vowel sounds. The second is that vowel sounds either precede or follow consonants and consonant blends, and make understandable words, speech, and language possible. The third is that the pronunciation of vowel sounds, especially those occurring in a later location within longer words, often sound much like those of other vowels, rather than being clearly pronounced to the degree that consonants and consonant blends are.

The following chart has been a useful first step in development of recommendations and in reaching the above conclusions.

1	2	3	4	5
L-L	L-S	L-L	L-S	L-L
A-A	A-A	A-E	A-E	A-I
E-A	E-A	E-E	E-E	E-I
I-A	I-A	I-E	I-E	I-I
O-A	O-A	O-E	O-E	O-I
U-A	U-A	U-E	U-E	U-I

6	7	8	9	10
L-S	L-L	L-S	L-L	L-S
A-I	A-O	A-O	A-U	A-U
E-I	E-O	E-O	E-U	E-U
I-I	I-O	I-O	I-U	I-U
O-I	O-O	O-O	O-U	O-U
U-I	U-O	U-O	U-U	U-U

The chart shows possible vowel combinations. The hyphen (-) between the letters is to confirm that each letter is to be pronounced separately.

The first letter in each of the combinations is given a long vowel pronunciation (L).

The second letters in the first, third, fifth, seventh and ninth columns are also given a long vowel pronunciation (L).

The five long vowel pronunciations determined to work best in "fluidity in sound" or smooth movement from long vowel sounds to related short vowel sounds are:

1. A, not as *Alpha* is now pronounced in English, but as a long A vowel sound, as in the words *about, farm, father,* and the German name *Bach.*

2. E, not as *Beta* is sometimes pronounced in English, but as a long E sound, as in the words *rein, vein,* and *skein.*

3. I, not as *Iota* is pronounced in English, but as I is used in *Lido* (Italian language), *Julius, lien,* and *ski.*

4. O, as used in the Greek letter *Omega,* and in the words *pony* and *lotus.*

5. U, as used in the Greek letter *Upsilon,* and in the words *lunar* and *duty.*

The second letters in the second, fourth, sixth, eighth and tenth columns are given the short vowel pronunciation (S). The five short vowel pronunciations are the same as the ones now used in the English language for A, E, I, O, and U in the words *bat, bet, bit, hot,* and *but.* (See again the earlier lists of words with these short vowel pronunciations.)

Again, the "fluidity in sound" movement, referred to earlier, occurs when speech is gliding from a long vowel sound to another long vowel sound, or to related short vowel sounds. It will be evident to language experts that the long vowel pronunciations that have been considered best in "sound fluidity" relationship to the five short vowel sounds in *bat, bet, bit, hot,* and *but* are the same as those in use in other Western languages.

THE REFINED CHART

It has been necessary to refine the chart in order to develop an orderly array of vowel sounds that can be used in the spelling of a large number of words, while retaining phonetic pronunciations.

1	2		3	4		5	6		7	8		9	10	
L'L	L-S		L'L	L-S		L'L	L-S		L'L	L-S		L'L	L-S	
A'A	A-A	AA	A'E	A-E		A'I	A-I	AI	AO	A-O		A'U	A-U	AU
EA	E-A		E'E	E-E	(EE)	E'I	E-I	EI	EO	E-O		E'U	E-U	EU
IA	I-A		I'E	I-E	IE	I'I	I-I		IO	I-O		I'U	IU	
OA	O-A		O'E	O-E	OE	O'I	O-I	OI	O'O	O-O	(OO)	O'U	O-U	OU
UA	U-A		U'E	U-E	UE	U'I	U-I		UO	U-O		U'U	U-U	

Again the first letters in each of the combinations in the numbered columns are given the long vowel pronunciation (L). The second letters in the first, third, fifth, seventh, and ninth columns are also given the long vowel pronunciation (L). The diacritic (') precedes the second letter in some of the combinations in these columns to emphasize that the second letter must be given the long vowel pronunciation (L) to ensure accuracy in pronunciation.

The second letters in the second, fourth, sixth, eighth, and tenth columns are given the short vowel pronunciation (S). The hyphen (-) precedes the second letter in all but one of the combinations in these columns to emphasize that the second letter must be given a short vowel pronunciation (S) to ensure accuracy in pronunciation. That one combination in the tenth column (IU) comes down from the Roman Empire era. Example: *Julius*.

Use of the diacritic (') and the hyphen (-), as shown in the columns, would be advisable to ensure phonetic pronunciations where needed and to avoid conflict with pronunciations of the vowel combinations discussed below.

THE 21 COMBINATIONS

Nine of these 21 combinations (shown again below) appear in the regular columns in the chart. Eight (4 in the first column and 4 in the seventh column) are reflections of the "fluidity in sound" necessary in gliding from a long vowel sound to another long vowel sound. The IU combination in the tenth column reflects similar "fluidity in sound" in gliding from a long I to a short U. These nine combinations can be used in spelling a large number of English words and names.

1	7	10
L'L	L'L	L-S
	AO	
EA	EO	
IA	IO	IU
OA		
UA	UO	

Twelve combinations (shown again below) are inserted between the numbered chart columns for use as particular vowel sounds. Five of these combinations are: AI as the vowel sound in *ait*, OI as in *coin*, AU as in *haul*, EU as in *feud*, and OU as in *out*. Five of the combinations are: AA as an alternative to ensure long A vowel sound, and the combinations EI, IE, OE, and UE for use in identifying long vowel pronunciation (as in *rein, lien, foe, sue*). Those four vowel combinations are already in use in a great number of English words, such as *vein, field, noel* and *duel*. Where "sound convenience" does not indicate correct pronunciation of ei, ie, oe, or ue, a diacritic or a hyphen would ensure correct pronunciation (as in *de-ity, si-esta, co-ed*, or *du-et*). The (OO) and (EE) combinations will be discussed later.

1	2		3	4		5	6		7	8		9	10	
	AA						AI							AU
			(EE)				EI							EU
			IE											
			OE				OI			(OO)				OU
			UE											

RECOMMENDED VOWEL PRONUNCIATIONS

As a result of examination of vowel usage and development of the refined chart, specific recommendations can be made for phonetic pronunciations of the vowels for 10 long and short vowel sounds.

I

1. Upper-case A (or use Aa) for a long A vowel sound at the beginning of names. Examples: *Adenauer (or use Aadenauer), Aden (or Aaden), A-gana.* (Note: Preceding R, the letter A is a long A vowel sound. Examples: *Arden, Arthur.*)
2. Upper-case A (or use Aa) for a long A vowel sound at the beginning of a sentence. Examples: *About, Along, A-way.*
3. Lower-case a (or use aa) for a long A vowel sound at the beginning of words in the middle of a sentence or in the middle of a word or name. Examples: *about, along, Bach, avoid, father.* (Note: In 1, 2, and 3 above, where long vowel pronunciation of A is more "sound convenient" than short vowel pronunciation, the AA is not needed.)
4. Lower-case a for a long A vowel sound second in vowel combinations. Examples: *goal, dual.*

II

1. Upper-case A for a short A vowel sound at the beginning of a name. Examples: *Andrew, Abner, Achison, Alvin.*
2. Upper-case A for a short A vowel sound at the beginning of a sentence. Examples: *After, Actors, At, Angry.*
3. Lower-case a for a single short A vowel sound at the beginning of words in the middle of a sentence or in the middle of a word or name. Examples: *sat, bandit, Banks, Hatch, actor, ant.*
4. Lower-case a for a short A vowel sound second in vowel combinations. Examples: *fi-at, co-axial.*

III, IV, V, VI

1. Upper-case E, I, O, or U (or use Ei, Ie, Oe, or Ue) for long vowel sounds at the beginning of names. Examples: *Eva, Ivar, Olson, O-wen, O-Hara, Ulrich, Omaha, O-Leary.*
2. Upper-case E, I, O, or U (or use Ei, Ie, Oe or Ue) for long vowel sounds at the beginning of sentences. Examples: *Over, Uber.*
3. Lower-case e, i, o, or u (or use ei, ie, oe, or ue) for long vowel sounds at the beginning of words in the middle of a sentence or

in the middle of words or names. Examples: *beta, Megan, Lisa, Jonas, onus, Boer, suer, uno.* (Note: In 1, 2, and 3 above, where long vowel pronunciation of E, I, O, or U is more "sound convenient" than short vowel pronunciation, the Ei, Ie, Oe, or Ue are not needed.)

4. Lower-case `e, `i, `o, `u for long vowel sounds second in vowel combinations. Examples: *A`ida, Hawai`i, co`itus, Kaho`olawe.*

VII, VIII, IX, X

1. Upper-case E, I, O, and U for short vowel sounds at the beginning of names. Examples: *Edward, Ilsa, Underwood, Oliver.*
2. Upper-case E, I, O, and U for short vowel sounds at the beginning of sentences. Examples: *Every, Impulse, Utter, Otter.*
3. Lower-case e, i, o, and u for short vowel sounds at the beginning of words in the middle of a sentence, or in the middle of words or names. Examples: *etch, itch, optical, under, letter, bitter, blunder, flop, Kennedy, Lott.* (Note: This short O vowel sound resembles the long A vowel sound.)
4. Lower-case -e, -i, and -o, for short vowel sounds second in vowel combinations. Examples: *co-educational, co-incidence, co-operative.*

The Aa, Ei, Ie, Oe, and Ue spelling options, shown above for the long vowels A, E, I, O, and U, are among the vowel combinations referred to earlier as among those most likely to be used in the spelling of words or names. Again, the others are ea, ia, oa, ua, ao, eo, io, uo, iu (as in *Julius*), ai, oi, au, eu, and ou.

It should be emphasized that when a, e, i, o, and u appear alone, following a consonant at the end of words or names, they would always receive the long vowel sound. Examples: *camera, Alabama, posse, passe, Mississippi, Henri, Li, bingo, macho, Peru, Chu.*

Regarding the long I, it would be acceptable to substitute Y for the long I at the end of words or names. Examples: *Billy, Kennedy, arche-ology, surly, boy.* However, any use of the Y in place of the I in the middle of words or names such as *bayou, Keynes, greyer,* or *Boyle* should be exercised with great care. This is necessary to avoid conflict with correct phonetic pronunciation of a Y serving as a consonant beginning a new syllable.

SIX MORE VOWEL SOUNDS

For the eleventh vowel sound, the medium length U vowel sound mentioned earlier, the symbol proposed is O with a line at an angle across it (Ø). Examples are *pøl, løk,* and *pøt* (now *pull, look,* and *put*).

One of the vowel combinations inserted in the chart is the AI, to be used as the long vowel sound in such spellings as *Hawai`i, ait,* and *hait* (now *height*). Regarding this AI long vowel sound, when the modern German language was developed, the vowel combination EI was chosen for this sound, as in the words *eins, zwei, drei* (*one, two, three*). The same vowel sound is in the name of the river *Main* and the city *Mainz;* this results in conflict in phonetic pronunciation of the letters A and E. The AI in *Main* and *Mainz* is more logical for this sound. The EI is best used as the long EI in *vein, rein, Leif Erikson,* and *skein.*

Four other combinations, mentioned earlier, are inserted in the chart for these vowel sounds:

1. OI (or oy) for the sound in *coin* or *Roy.*
2. AU (or aw) for the sound in *haul* or *awl.*
3. EU for the sound in *feud* or *Europa.*
4. OU (or ow) for the sound in *scout* or *bower.*

The use of W in place of U in the AU and OU combinations can be acceptable. However, this too should be exercised with great care, to avoid conflict with phonetic pronunciation where a following syllable begins with W as a consonant. Then, for phonetic accuracy, the W should be preceded by a hyphen as in *O-wen* or *a-way.*

As noted earlier, correct short vowel pronunciation of a, e, i, o, or u is assisted when they precede a doubling of the same consonant. Examples: *batting, setter, biggest, otter, Ott, butter.*

THE OO AND EE COMBINATIONS

It has been tempting to propose continued use of more of the vowel combinations now in English language use, so as to offer a somewhat wider array of vowel pronunciations and spellings than is recommended herein. To do so, however, would simply result in inconsistency of vowel duplication of pronunciation of other vowels, and defeat the effort to gain concise phonetic pronunciation of vowels and vowel combinations. Consequently, only two of these vowel pronunciations have been inserted in the chart.

The OO combination has been included, not only because of its long time use in the English language as an alternative to the recommended long U and long UE sounds (as in such words as *soon, loose, hoot, boot, coot* and *shoot*), but also because the OO combination can be readily distinguished from the other long U and long UE sounds. Also, the O`O and O-O can be used where needed to clarify pronunciation, as in *Kaho`olawe* and *co-operation*.

The EE combination has been included in the chart for two reasons. It has had long time use in many words in the English language (such as *seen, queen, heed, reel,* and *feel)* and possesses the same long vowel sound as that of the long I (or IE) used in such words as *siege, lien, fiend,* and *chief.* Consequently, use of EE as an alternate for IE is recommended. The diacritic or hyphen can be used to clarify pronunciation, if needed for E`E and E-E.

THE K (Q) SITUATION

The letter (Q) following K in the list of consonants is the same consonant sound as the K. Therefore, use of the (Q) as an alternative K requires explanation. Beginning with Latin and carrying down into modern European languages, the (Q) has been used in combination with the letter U (the U being pronounced like W). An example is the Latin word *aqueduct.* Therefore, continuing limited use in English of the QU combination appears acceptable. Uses proposed are qualm (or *quaalm) quak, queint, quest, queen, quit, quoeta, quot, quait,* and *quai-et.*

However, there is need for correct pronunciation of U following other consonants, especially G, which is closely related to K, e.g. *Guatemala, guano, Guam, Kuomintang.* In other instances, a need exists to press for the use of W instead of U to advance phonetic pronunciation and precise spelling. This is exemplified in *bwana, Kwai, swing, Zwingli, dwell, Kwantung.*

CONCISE USE OF VOWELS

Concise use of vowel sounds in support of consonants and consonant blends is essential to phonetic pronunciation. This is especially true for vowels or vowel combinations that may precede or follow one of the nine consonant blends: x (ks), c (ts), ch (tsh), the non-voiced th, hw, sh, and the voiced th, ng, zh.

Excepting W, H, and Y, the consonants listed earlier can either precede or follow any of the 16 vowel sounds (11 vowel sounds and 5 combination vowel sounds). The W, H, and Y consonants must be used with care.

In some instances W can be substituted for U in the vowel sound combinations au and ou. W can precede the ai, au, and ou vowel combinations, and the ei as well, but not the eu combination. W should not follow any of the five combinations.

H may precede the vowel sound combinations ai, oi, au, eu and ou, and the ei as well, but it should not follow any of them. Use of H following vowel sounds should be very limited, e. g. O-Hara and a-hoy.

Y can be substituted for i in the vowel sound combinations ai and oi (and in ei as well). Y can precede the vowel combinations ai, oi, au, and ou, and the ei as well but it should not precede eu. To indicate emphasis, y may in some instances follow the vowel sounds aw and ow.

ADVANTAGES

There are several advantages to the above recommendations for vowels and vowel combinations. First, continuing use of the first of the long A pronunciations now used in English ensures the "fluidity in sound" already in use in English in the names and words *Laos, Maori, boa, goal, foal,* and *Mao.* The recommended long E provides "fluidity in sound" and takes care of *Meo* (the Meo people of Asia), *rein, Leif,* and *Leonardo,* and the recommended long I provides "fluidity in sound" for *lien, siege, ski, fiend,* and *Rio.*

Some readers of this essay might support continued use of the present English language long vowel pronunciations of E and I, and oppose the recommended use of EI and IE, as in *vein* and *lien.* While continued use of the present long E and I pronunciations might at first glance appear desirable, they would require change from the recommended long E (EI) vowel pronunciation at the ends of *passe* and *posse,* and from the long I (IE) pronunciations at the ends of *Missouri, Mississippi, Andretti,* and *Pelosi.* Changing the long Y (a substitute for I or IE) at the ends of *Kennedy, Kerry,* and *Harry* to make long Y a substitute for E might appear easy.

However, continuing the present long E and I pronunciations would present more significant problems. It would be necessary to change the present long vowel IE spelling and pronunciation in *lien*, *thief*, and *chief* to long EE as in *cheef* and *theef*, and change the present spellings in *vein*, *rein*, *seine*, *Keynes*, *Leif*, and *convey*.

In contrast the proposals in this essay allow continued use of the E (EI) in *vein*, *Leif*, *rein*, and *seine*. They allow continued use of the EU combination in *feud*, along with improved spellings in *beuty*, *feul*, and *heu*. They allow the longtime use of IU in *Julius* and *Cassius* to continue, along with improved spellings that could be made to such words as *gracius* and *luxurius*. They allow continued use of the long I at the end of *Missouri* and *Pelosi* and the substitution of Y for the long I at the end of *Kennedy*, *boy*, *coy*, etc.

The recommended long vowel pronunciations of E (or EI), I (or IE), and the AI combination are "sound convenient" and would relate well with European languages. This seems to be true also for translations from languages in other areas of the world as well. English now smoothly provides *rein*, *vein*, *lien*, *siege*, *dual*, *patio*, and *thief* without the use of a diacritic to indicate pronunciation of the second vowel in such combinations. Also, English already makes use of such words and names as *passe*, *ait*, *hait* (present *height*), *Hawai`i*, *coin*, *coy*, *ay* (*yes*), *haul*, *awl*, *bout*, *cow*, and *feud*.

LONG OR SHORT VOWEL PRONUNCIATIONS

Where a single E vowel appears within a word or name with no doubled consonant following (as in *well*), a question can be raised as to whether the vowel should be given a long or short pronunciation, e.g., *Megan*, *Las Vegas*, *La-redo*, and *Regan*. If long vowel pronunciation of the E is more "sound convenient" and more common than short vowel pronunciation, there is no need for substituting an EI combination. The same principle may in some instances be applied to other single vowels at the beginning of or within a word or name. However, if there is uncertainty about pronunciation, to ensure long vowel pronunciation the AA, EI, IE, OE, and UE vowel combinations should be used.

Therefore, the argument for the vowel pronunciations recommended in this essay is that they provide concise phonetic pronunciations, "fluidity in sound", and "speech convenience". Speakers of languages instinctively desire these characteristics. English language grammar is said to be one of the most easily learned and used in the world; its spelling and pronunciation ought to continue moving in that direction. Concise phonetic pronunciations and precise spellings would make English more easily taught, more clearly spoken, and more efficiently used in cursive writing, word processing, and publishing, thus providing an example for improvement in phonetic pronunciations and word spellings for other languages.

POSSIBLE OBJECTIONS

Objections can be raised to the apparently extensive use in both the Refined Chart and in the Recommended Vowels of the diacritic (`) to indicate correct long vowel pronunciations and the use of the hyphen (-) to indicate correct short vowel pronunciations. However, re-examination of the Refined Chart will reveal that neither a diacritic nor hyphen appears in the 21 combinations most likely to be used in the spelling of words or names -- and to be remembered without the guidance of a diacritic or hyphen.

Also, re-examination of the listings of Recommended Vowels will reveal that the diacritic or hyphen are needed, mainly for clarifying the pronunciation of vowels or vowel combinations that are not commonly used in words or names.

Some of the necessary exceptions are as follows: Use of the hyphen in such words as *co-axial, co-education, co-incidence, co-operative, si-esta, du-et, fi-at,* and *de-ity* is essential to avoid conflict with the recommended long vowel sounds (including OO) and the smooth pronunciations in the ea, ia, oa, ua, ei, ie, oe, ue, ao, eo, io, uo, and the ai and oi combinations.

Also, "sound convenience" as well as a properly used diacritic or hyphen can become the determinant, where needed, for correct phonetic pronunciation of the first syllable in a word or the most significant syllable in an unfamiliar multi-syllable word, e.g. *Vi-etnam, Fuku-oka* in *Ja-pan, O-wen, pro-gram, Bra-zil, O-saka,* and *Naga-saki.*

However, neither a diacritic nor hyphen will solve one problem; single vowels in the second syllables of words or names often are pronounced by speakers so as to be difficult to distinguish. For example, note the second vowel in the spelling of *Kennedy* or *Kennady, Mullen* or *Mullin,* and *Moffet, Moffit,* or *Moffat.*

Referring to the possible combinations of consonants and consonant blends discussed earlier, some languages appear to combine consonants in combinations in which an intervening vowel or hyphen would appear to be helpful; yet none is indicated. For example, the first Gb in the name *Gbog-ba* (recently in news from Africa), the Gd in *Gdansk*, and the gn in *gnu*.

MAKING LANGUAGE A BETTER TOOL

Working to determine and clarify pronunciation and use of the 18 consonants and 9 consonant blends, and to develop precise phonetics and spelling for the 11 vowel sounds and the 5 commonly used vowel-symbol combinations (AI, OI, AU, EU, and OU) in the English language, has led to this conclusion. Alphabets, word spellings, and written languages have throughout written human history evolved primarily as an attempted imitation of vocal sounds; these have been set down with insufficient effort exerted to make language a more precise tool. Hopefully the efforts reviewed in this essay can be used by language experts to use consonants, consonant blends, vowels, and vowel combinations to improve and advance phonetic pronunciation and concise spelling of words and names to make language the precise tool that humans deserve.

Humans believe completely in the value of precision in numbers. It is logical, therefore, to seek concise phonetic pronunciations for consonants, consonant blends, vowels, and vowel combinations. Doing so would lead toward more precise language, for English and for other languages. A consortium of language experts in the English-speaking world could take the lead, by working toward a higher degree of uniformity in phonetic pronunciations of consonants, consonant blends, vowels, and vowel combinations, to improve the spelling of words in the English language. Similar consortiums could do the same for Western European languages, the Central and Eastern European languages, and major languages all around the world. The result would be greater ease in learning to pronounce, read, speak, and write the languages of other peoples. Improved ease of translation and communication between peoples would be a strong step forward for humanity.

Language experts are capable of developing concise phonetic pronunciation and spelling of words for languages, while still maintaining and even improving the necessary tools of grammar: subjects, nouns, adjectives, pronouns, genders, plurals, singulars, verbs, adverbs, tense, objects, etc. It would take thought and work on the part of language experts, but it would be worthwhile and such effort should be supported by every major nation.

The first step in this direction could be efforts to either respell or create new words to replace the numerous English words containing illogical phonetics and spelling (e.g., *lieu, ought, height, reign, beau, through, draught, tough, playwright, wrong*) and inconsistent pronunciations (e.g., *mint* and *pint*). Another could be respelling of words to eliminate the "silent" or unpronounced E following a consonant at the end of many English words (e.g., *rude, rote, late, cede,* and *kite*). In such words as *walked* and *bartered,* English speakers through "speech convenience" have already replaced the Old English ED ending with a T sound in the first word, and a D sound in the second; this has not occurred with such words as *bonded* or *tinted.* Modern-day spelling should more accurately reflect this phonetic change.

Such changes may seem challenging, but English dictionaries now contain many words having more than one meaning. For example: *list, miss, left, kit, foul, fast, dock,* and *trunk.* Although such words have the same spelling (and the same pronunciation) they differ in meaning due to the contexts in which they are used. Also, dictionaries which are guides to accurate pronunciation, spelling, meaning, and use of words could be simplified by the use, where necessary, of diacritics and hyphens in written language. Some words already in dictionaries could receive more use than they do now, if their spelling were more reflective of their actual pronunciation.

Where inconvenience has led to incorrect pronunciation of a vowel, as in such words as *covenant* and *love,* a change in spelling to a more "sound convenient" vowel would ensure phonetic pronunciation and accurate spelling. The spellings of personal and family names might also be improved. Examples: *Jon, Wein or Weyn, Ralf, Andru, Deil or Deyl,* and *Loyd* (now *John, Wayne, Ralph, Andrew, Dale,* and *Lloyd*).

Another desirable action would be to apply precise gender (masculine, feminine, neuter) to persons and objects in the German language where one must now memorize the odd and unpredictable gender of every noun. (That would be a blessing not only for non-native students of that language, but for native German speakers, as well.) Surely that could be accomplished by German language experts in global concert with language experts intent on refining world languages.

For those who appreciate the global importance of geography and history, it would be extremely useful to find uniformity in the spellings of the names of all geographical physical features, places, and areas -- and the names of historical personalities, groups, and nations. It would not be difficult to use more desirable names for each of these four cities now known locally as *Köln* (with an umlaut O), *Pari(s)*, *Roma,* and *Wien,* but now known in English as *Cologne, Paris, Rome,* and *Vienna;* the alternate spellings of *Køln* (with a line across the o), *Pari, Roma,* and *Vien* would more closely approximate the way native speakers pronounce these names. The study of geography and history might be less difficult if uniform spellings and pronunciations of names and titles were available for use by geographers, historians, and journalists around the world.

There is no doubt that language experts are capable of developing a high degree of uniformity in symbols for concise phonetic pronunciation of the sounds in speech, precision in word spellings, and improvements in grammar in the major languages. Their efforts in doing so would be a great step forward in global communication. The end result would be deeper and broader understanding and more friendly relations between groups of people and nations throughout the world.

DDC

SETTLEMENTS AND BOUNDARIES

AN ESSAY
BY DALE D. CANNADY

The significance of boundaries first became evident to me during college studies concerning the physical world and the history of human occupation of the Earth. No doubt, my employment by municipalities, and work in city planning, led to increased awareness concerning the importance of boundaries and settlements. Observing the world news and the workings of government organizations at all levels advanced my knowledge and appreciation for the desirability of well-located boundaries. The purpose of this essay is to offer a methodology for improvement of designated jurisdictional boundaries at all levels of government. To do so, it is helpful to understand how both human settlements and their governmental organizations originally came into existence.

SETTLEMENTS DEFINED

A settlement may be defined as a concentration of humans, their shelters, and their possessions, surrounding a core area of commercial and personal service facilities. A settlement supports the advantages and pleasures of social contacts, including the commercial and personal services, which can be provided to the residents of the settlement, the residents of a surrounding area, and persons traveling to or through the settlement. It makes possible the creation of an organization to provide security and necessary support services for the residents and businesses.

Settlements vary in size in relation to the number of people who can and will rely on the contacts and services that the settlement can make available to them. It should be noted that a facility, providing very limited commercial or personal service to a very small number of people within an immediately adjacent area and/or to persons traveling past the facility, does not meet the definition of a settlement, as set forth above.

The organizations created by governments to provide security and support services for settlements are called municipalities. Municipalities govern areas within specific jurisdictional boundaries, and are the lowest level of governmental organization. Next in the hierarchy of governmental organizations are districts and provinces; in the United States these are called counties and states. The top level is the nation-state; the United States is one of these.

The land areas, and to some extent the water surfaces, of the Earth are included within the boundaries of governmental jurisdictions. In some instances, governmental boundaries are located within stream courses, or in lakes or bays. By international agreement, nation-states bounded by seas or oceans may extend their jurisdictional boundaries into those water bodies.

Often, however, the existing jurisdictional boundaries of nation-states, provinces, and districts are not located along what might be considered the most advantageous geographical lines. Political and cultural divisions have disrupted what could have led to logical divisions based on geographical realities and man's original rationale when selecting sites for settlements. Therefore, it is first necessary to review how settlements came into being.

HUMAN ORIGINS AND MIGRATION

Settlements began coming into existence, as small groups of humans began to occupy the Earth long ago. The locations of those settlements were determined by physical geography: sites offering security, ease of access to and from locations, and availability of water and food sources. Anthropologists and archaeologists tell us that human occupation of the world began in Sub-Saharan Africa. Anthropologists continue to find skeleton fragments of our ancestors in that portion of the world, and are able to date human origins to between three and four million years ago.

The urge to survive, both as individuals and as groups, has been necessary for continued human existence. That urge, the desire to explore, and the competitive spirit of both human ancestors and humans, led to the migrations that populated most of the Earth's land area.

No consensus exists among anthropologists, regarding the timing and precise pattern of human occupation of the Earth's land areas. However, based on known differences among humans, there appear to have been two very early human migrations from Sub-Saharan Africa across Southwestern Asia and into tropical India, Southeastern Asia, and Melanesia. Anthropologists estimate that one early human migration extended into Australia as much as 40,000 to 50,000 years ago.

Following the migrations into Southwestern, Southern, and Southeastern Asia, humans migrated northward long ago into Europe and Eastern Asia. The descendants of migration into Eastern Asia are known as Mongoloids; the descendants of migration into Europe are known as Caucasoids.

Reports by anthropologists concerning human ancestors in Europe have them gradually replacing the Neanderthals who preceded them in Europe. The migration of humans northward into Europe must have begun at least 60,000 years ago. Groups similar to the Neanderthals may have preceded the arrival of humans into Eastern Asia.

The successful migrations of Mongoloid and Caucasoid ancestors could not have proceeded far into the northern areas of the Eurasian land mass until humans:

1. Developed the use of furs and weaving.
2. Mastered the use of fire.
3. Learned how to preserve foods.
4. Used caves or constructed shelters.

These skills were necessary to survive the cold winter temperatures of the northern areas of Europe and Eastern Asia.

At least as far back as the end of the last ice age, about 13,500 to 18,000 years ago, and perhaps earlier, Mongoloids migrated from Northeastern Asia, either by sea or via a Bering Sea land bridge, into North America. Eventually that migration proceeded into Central and South America. Recent information suggests that there may also have been a migration by sea from Western Europe into Eastern North America.

A reverse Caucasoid migration from Europe, southeasterly into areas south of Central Eurasia and then into India, began 5,000 to 6,000 years ago. Mongoloids, already merged with Southeastern Asians, began their migration into Oceania (the islands in the Pacific Ocean) and later to New Zealand and Hawaii at least 1,500 years ago; this migration must have followed an earlier Mongoloid migration southward from Eastern Asia into Southeastern Asia.

Within the large areas of land settled by humans, there have been, and continue to be only superficial differences in human appearance -- what are sometimes considered racial differences. Those superficial physical differences among human migratory groups are adaptations selected for survival in response to particular geographic locales.

Where the most noticeable differences in human appearance locally exist, they are the result of either racial discrimination and genetic isolation (e.g. against the Bushmen and Pygmies in Africa) or geographical isolation (e.g. the Aborigines who entered Australia long ago). Isolation similar to that of the Australian Aborigines may have happened to the Ainu people, the remainder of whom are located in northern Japan. The differences in human physical appearance in the three major areas of the Earth (Europe, Eastern Asia, and Sub-Saharan Africa) appear to be due to continued isolation from further in-migration, as well as continued adaptation over time. Changes in environment and climate prompted further adaptations in human appearance.

THE ORIGIN OF SETTLEMENTS

All the human migrations discussed above were accomplished by exploration, selection of sites for secure outposts, and then by the establishment of settlements, providing security and shelter for members of groups. Sites for pre-historic settlements, whether temporary or permanent, must have been selected with four geographical considerations in mind:

1. Sites offering the best possible security.
2. Availability of water.
3. Availability of food through hunting, fishing, and plant gathering.
4. Locations near travel and transport routes.

At first security from predatory animals was a primary consideration.

Later, security from competitive human groups became more significant.

The same considerations were important in recent centuries, as Europeans and their descendants expanded their areas of occupation across the Americas -- first with groups of explorers, then with hunting groups, then with trading posts and forts, and finally with frontier settlements.

Site selection and choice of travel and transport routes have determined the pattern of human migration and the development of settlements that began long ago. Critical to settlement locations and development patterns have been the geographical factors of landforms, water bodies and streams, climate, soils, natural vegetation, and animal life.

Travel and transport routes were important from the beginning. Until recent times, humans selected routes for convenience as to physical terrain, availability of water, types of vegetation, and general direction and distance to an expected destination. European expansion across the American continents required routes having these same characteristics. Technology available at the time governed use of navigable water routes.

ORGANIZATION WITHIN SETTLEMENTS

From their beginning, human migrations and settlements required leadership decisions and actions. Their continued success depended on organization and management. Group and clan leaders first, and then tribal chiefs, with the support of shamans or priests/medicine men, set policies, rules, and behavioral ethics for their followers. As time passed and population growth occurred, competition between groups made security needs and economic considerations increasingly important. Even among primitive peoples, economic resources and entrepreneurial action eventually came to be more than means for survival, and the economic power and wealth of some individuals and sub-groups grew.

At the same time, war leaders became more influential, sharing in power and wealth. War leaders managed conflicts between groups, clans, and tribes over the control of areas containing food resources, water resources, secure routes of movement, defensive situations, and the physical and economic security of the group. Physical, linguistic, and religious differences among humans have enhanced these conflicts throughout history.

THE RISE OF TOWN AND CITY STATES

Early written history reveals the rise of town states, guided by leaders or so-called kings who, with trusted powerful subordinates and the aid of war leaders, controlled one or more towns and the populated surrounding countryside. Some of these towns may have grown large enough to be considered small cities.

Later, coalitions of town and city-states provided temporary security and/or economic prosperity. An early example is the coalition of town and city-states in ancient Palestine, caught between the Egyptians to the south, the Hittites to the north, and the Sea People (perhaps the early Greeks) along the Mediterranean Sea coast. Because Palestine provided a weak power base, these coalitions accepted alliances and changed sides, as power shifted from one to another of their stronger neighbors.

The first small nation-states came into existence in the major river valleys of the Nile, Tigris/Euphrates, Indus, and major rivers of North China. Knowledge about these early nation states continues to increase through the efforts of archeologists, who excavate ancient building sites, and linguists, who examine and translate ancient writings. Increasingly large nation-states were forced to divide their territories for administrative purposes into districts (counties) and provinces (states).

ECONOMIC COMPETITION AND
GROWTH OF SETTLEMENTS

Human settlements grew in number, where physical resources existed for the sustenance of larger populations, each facing economic competition from their nearest neighbors. To the present time, settlements remain few in number, or non-existent, in the coldest, driest, hottest, swampiest, and most mountainous areas of the Earth. Settlements are greatest in number in choice areas where climate, good soils, adequate water, and ease of transport and travel have made agricultural production, population growth, commerce, and survival easiest.

The smallest settlements are commonly called villages. Larger settlements are called towns. Both villages and towns provide commercial and personal services to the residents of their settlement, as well as the residents of the surrounding rural area. In areas of very high population density, villages and towns may be located as little as 2 or 3 miles apart. In areas of very low population density, the distance to the nearest village or town may be many miles.

A larger population concentration, which may be defined as a city, has one or more important local commercial and personal service centers, clearly distinct from the principal commercial service center of the urban concentration. Such local commercial centers may be either one or more villages or towns overgrown by the city's expanding urbanized area, or one or more commercial centers that have grown up to meet the desire for services in areas of additional city residential growth. Most large cities contain old competitor settlements that have been overgrown. Large cities may even grow to adjoin. Seattle and Tacoma, Washington, are one example.

OTHER GROWTH FACTORS

Competition between villages, towns, and cities focuses on the services provided to both residents of the settlement and the residents of surrounding rural areas. However, in some instances growth has been stimulated by other factors. Some settlements have grown where valuable natural resources exist: lumber, minerals, stone, gems, mineral waters, oil, natural gas, coal, and animal and fish resources. In some instances, these resources have helped to stimulate growth into a city (e.g. Johannesburg, South Africa -- originally a gold mining center). However, for some settlements substantial growth has been followed by decline and decay, because the resource that was the reason for their beginning was exhausted or declined in value (e.g. ghost towns in Western United States).

Settlement growth has been particularly strong at land or water transport and travel route junctions, as well as crew change or servicing locations. Some of these have declined in value later. Examples are the ancient city of Ephesus in Turkey, whose harbor filled with silt, and the decline of Chester, England as a port, due to silting of the Dee River estuary and the rise of Liverpool as a competing seaport.

Manufacturing has risen and declined in differing locations as resources have been consumed or technology has changed. Military forts and posts, and naval bases as well, have increased and declined in importance and size, as location desirability and need changed due to technological and competitive influences.

In recent times, two factors have been reliable indicators of continued existence and growth of towns and cities. First, colleges and universities, once established, generally remain fixed locations within towns and cities. Second, once a town becomes a government center, its growth usually outstrips competing centers. This has occurred even when competitive towns may have been more advantageously located for growth. Provincial and district government service centers generally remain solidly fixed, once sited. In modern times, national governmental service centers (capitol cities) have led to great urban population growth.

GROWTH AND IMPORTANCE OF GOVERNMENTS

Almost from the beginning of human settlements, there has been some form of organization to provide governmental services for the people residing within the organization's jurisdiction. Governments provide for the physical and personal security of persons and their goods, and either directly or indirectly for their economic, social, and informational contacts and needs.

Throughout pre-historical and historical times, humans have created, abandoned or destroyed, re-created, and modified governments and governmental service areas. In most instances, governments themselves have played a key role in these changes.

The most famous historical leaders are remembered primarily because of their close involvement with governments and governmental service areas. Most people remember able rulers, kings, presidents, prime ministers, powerful legislators, and prominent judges more than leaders in other fields of service, with three possible exceptions. Those are especially able war leaders, generals and admirals, in wars between governments; leaders who founded or advanced major religious movements that have impacted governments and governmental service areas; and people whose work led either to significant technological advancement, artistic recognition, or greater economic power and wealth from commercial activities.

GOVERNMENT OF SETTLEMENTS (MUNICIPALITIES)

Governmental organization is basic to the establishment and continuation of urban life for humans. In villages, towns, and cities, as with any successful human organization, there must be policymaking; record keeping; research, analysis and legal counsel; finance and support services; and operations. All require managers and employees.

A key action in creating a successful settlement is establishment of a government organization and the boundaries of its jurisdiction. In the United States a municipal government is established by means of a charter for incorporation approved by a higher level of government: a province (state) or a nation-state.

A successful municipal government must control the subdivision of contiguous tracts of land (both initially for the settlement area, and later for subsequent expansions) in order to provide an orderly pattern of building sites, streets for transportation, and pedestrian walkways. Land subdivision is most advantageous when blocks, lots, streets, and service alleys are laid out in a gridiron pattern adjusted to fit the land terrain. This ensures convenient access to and from blocks and lots, and minimizes engineering and construction problems in provision of water and other service lines.

Provision of access routes, urban water supply, sewage, and waste disposal are essential municipal services. Then fire protection and police protection are necessary for the security of both residents and businesses, and their possessions. Services, such as street lighting and mass transit lines, become necessary as the area and population of the settlement increase in size.

Over time, in settlements of significant size, construction permits, business licenses, nuisance abatement, and inspection and enforcement activities have become a customary part of local governmental actions. These protect consumers, public safety, and public health. Social services and amenities, such as parks and playgrounds, libraries, museums, theaters, arenas, and stadiums, have grown in importance more recently.

MODERN DAY CITY PLANNING AND BOUNDARIES

City planning, including residential, commercial, and industrial land use planning and zoning regulation, gained importance in cities in the United States between the early 1900s and World War II, growing greatly in status and scope since then. Land use planning and zoning regulation are most effective when the land uses allowed within zones are well selected and defined, the boundaries between zones are well located, and the integrity of the zones is well maintained. Unfortunately, city planning has not always included balanced integration of land use planning and transportation planning.

City planning tries to emphasize boundary delineation for residential areas, termed neighborhoods and communities (groups of neighborhoods). This has proceeded in cooperation with urban residents and school district management, to set service area boundaries for elementary, middle or junior high schools, and senior high schools. Coordination with park department management, for provision of neighborhood and community park/recreational facilities for the same service areas, has made urban living more desirable. City planning includes the location and boundaries of the principal city commercial center, the local commercial service centers, and the industrial areas of cities.

Travel and transport routes, including those for mass transit where there are large populations, are major elements in cities and towns. However, planning by transportation agencies themselves, for the location of transportation routes, continues to have a greater impact on the location of commercial service centers and the distribution of residential development, than has city planning for land use areas (zones) and the boundaries of communities and neighborhoods.

City planning is more advantageous when the focus on land use planning and planning for intra-city transportation routes is balanced. Then transportation planning becomes more clearly focused on provision of transportation facilities and services along routes connecting commercial centers and other key city areas. The intra-city routes subsequently serve as the boundaries of residential neighborhoods and communities. Only local streets should carry traffic into and out of residential neighborhoods, including schools and park/recreation facilities located within those neighborhoods.

This balanced approach to transportation planning and land use planning and regulation (zoning) would help to concentrate development and expansion of commercial centers at the most advantageous locations, and could help to control the haphazard location of new centers and the extension of "business ribbons". It could also help to discourage the location or expansion within residential neighborhoods of small commercial centers which are little more than "spot zones" (a land use planning and zoning term denoting illegality, and not often used now).

A more balanced approach could provide a strong basis for planning the location of different residential densities. Higher density residential development would be limited to planned locations abutting commercial centers and be restricted from locations within the lower density residential areas of neighborhoods and communities. Mixed commercial-residential use would be appropriate within commercial centers.

This approach would also clearly recognize two things. First, the size of commercial centers varies based upon their location and the size of their service areas. Second, their service areas are the adjoining neighborhood and community residential areas containing school and park/recreation facilities and services. Neither neighborhood elementary schools nor community high schools should ever be expected to be of uniform size; location and physical geography negate uniformity in their service areas. The locations for transportation routes, neighborhood commercial centers, and community commercial centers should be planned with regard to the physical setting of the urban area.

Industrial areas, regional parks, and high attendance facilities in larger settlements are best located with recognition of the physical geographic features of the urban area. Then transportation routes should be located to serve such areas and facilities.

GOVERNMENTS OF COUNTIES (DISTRICTS)

Nation-states typically divide their territories into districts and provinces for efficient administrative services. Districts are the first level of governmental jurisdiction above that of settlements. The United States uses the term county to denote a district; counties contain both settlements (villages, towns, or cities) and the rural areas that receive commercial and personal services from the settlements.

While police protection, jails, and municipal courts have long been features of incorporated settlements (municipalities), the more significant security function of police (county sheriff), county jail, lawful prosecution of crimes, and the primary level of judicial and court personnel (their duties and procedures) were long ago placed within the county jurisdictions. Counties include both settlements and rural areas.

In the United States, counties have long been responsible for the provision and maintenance of roads serving the rural areas outside municipalities. In recent times, counties have been increasingly engaged in the provision of public health and related human services and the provision of county parks, libraries, and museums.

Within county areas outside incorporated municipalities, land subdivision into streets and building sites; land use planning and zoning regulation; the granting of permits for buildings and septic tanks; and formation of water and fire protection districts have come to the fore in recent time. Thus, county governments have encouraged urban growth outside the jurisdictional boundaries of incorporated villages, towns, and cities, creating conflict and disorder in provision of governmental services. The willingness of municipalities to provide municipal water service to new urban development areas beyond their jurisdictional boundaries, without requiring annexation of such areas to their municipal jurisdiction, has aggravated the problem.

In the United States, there is real need to firm up the responsibilities and improve the relationships between counties and the municipalities (settlements) located within them. One alternative is for the United States and its states to enact laws placing more concise distinctions between the functions of the governments of municipalities (settlements) and counties, and then to prohibit county governments from engaging in governmental actions and services which are competitive with and harmful to effective performance by the municipalities. In turn, the governmental services of the municipalities would be limited to the area of their jurisdictions, with appropriate geographical location and expansion of those areas occurring only after study indicated the need for and suitable location of such growth. A suitable, state-prescribed lawful process should govern such expansions.

A second and less complicated alternative would be to eliminate municipal governments of settlements and place all local governmental services under county jurisdictions. This would make county governments fully responsible for the provision of governmental services within the entire county, in both settlements and the rural areas surrounding them.

State governments should be responsible for allowing the establishment of a new settlement within a county, only after study determines a need for such settlement, and after determining that the financial investors proposing establishment of a settlement can and will make the expenditures necessary to accommodate occupation by commercial entrepreneurs and residents. Then county governments could take responsibility, under state supervision, for controlling the boundaries and growth of settlements under their jurisdiction.

One advantage to this alternative could be the elimination of another level of government, a metropolitan government organization such as that established some time ago in the three-county area including both Portland, Oregon, and other smaller municipalities. The most significant power of the metropolitan government is control of the growth of the boundaries of the settlements within the Portland metropolitan area. State governance could easily transfer that control to a county government, eliminating one layer of bureaucratic organization within the metropolitan area.

RURAL LAND USE

It is generally recognized that agricultural land should be conserved to ensure food for future generations. State governance should allow counties to permit the establishment of a very limited commercial service, a resource development, or a very limited industrial operation within a rural area, only after study has clearly established a need at the location proposed. Such facility should be allowed only in conjunction with, and secondary to, an existing customary rural activity on a customarily sized rural property. No subdivision of land that would initiate a new settlement should be allowed, until state government has completed a study and determined that a new settlement is needed.

SCHOOL DISTRICTS

In the United States, private organizations continue to operate some schools for children and teenagers through high school. However, with the great increase in knowledge during the last two centuries, education of children and teenagers has become of much greater importance to citizens. The result is that such education is now accomplished primarily by school districts, another local governmental organization. Because school districts can serve the residents of both settlements and rural areas, they are separated from the governments of both municipalities and counties. However, these school organizations might better be placed directly under the jurisdiction of the counties, rather than being separate districts. School executives might be more responsive to county management than to a school district board.

IMPROVEMENT OF COUNTY (DISTRICT) BOUNDARIES

The boundaries between counties (districts) in the United States often have been arbitrarily drawn, because higher government has viewed counties simply as minor administrative areas. Often local political maneuvering has influenced the locations of boundaries and sizes of counties. This has resulted in the provision of numerous elective positions and appointive positions (both are political).

Most of the 48 states of the continental United States were divided into counties long before modern methods of transportation came into being. The result, particularly in the states in eastern parts of the United States, was division into small counties based to a great extent on how far people could conveniently travel by horse-drawn vehicles, or if necessary on foot, to the county governmental center.

Examination of the present boundaries of counties in the 48 continental states suggests that the boundaries and service areas of counties could be improved. Many states have an excessive number of smaller counties with poorly drawn boundaries. State governments could combine many of these smaller counties into larger counties with well-drawn boundaries. For example, the State of Nebraska could reduce its 93 counties by half or more.

Reducing the number of counties could result in more effective government at substantially lower cost to taxpayers. County government could also be improved by replacing the present legislative/executive commissions (usually 3 or 5 members) with policy-making bodies made up of representatives elected by the eligible voters within segments of the counties, and then having a county-wide election of a county executive (or county mayor) to serve as executive manager.

Geographical factors and population density should govern the size of counties. Some counties may easily extend 50 to 80 miles into thinly populated mountainous or desert areas, with most of the population located in only one part of the county. In such a county, the town having the most successful commercial service center could serve as the headquarters or management center for government services within the county area.

Some of those governmental services might have to be provided in subordinate outlying locations. Those are services that must be provided directly to specific individuals or groups within the county population. Cost for these services would be offset by the savings gained in increased efficiency in headquarters management, record keeping, and those governmental services that most residents of counties seldom need on a face-to-face basis.

In more densely populated areas, counties of smaller geographical area can be acceptable, because of the greater number of people to be served and the greater scale of services to be rendered. A large town or city can serve as the location for the governmental headquarters in such a county.

In any delineation of counties and their boundaries, consideration should be given not only to the boundaries of settlements but also to the adjoining rural areas to which each of the settlements provides commercial services. As noted earlier, settlements are competing with each other and each settlement varies in size in relation to the size of the rural area it serves.

In addition, because conditions can change over time, county boundaries and county headquarters locations should never be considered permanent, and should be subject to periodic review and adjustment.

GOVERNMENTS OF STATES (PROVINCES)

Districts (or counties) are necessary subdivisions of larger areas. Nation-states of small geographical area may need to divide their territories only into districts (or counties). However, nation-states with very large land areas and long internal distances have found it necessary to divide their territories into provinces, that may measure hundreds of miles across, before dividing the provinces into districts (counties). In the United States, provinces are termed states.

In very large nation-states, such as the United States, geography and the customs, and attitudes of the population may vary from province to province (state to state), to the extent that state or provincial governments need to be allowed some laws applicable only within their lower level jurisdiction, plus a necessary state (or province) court system. Nation-states of smaller geographical area, but with relatively large populations, may have sufficient differences within them to require similar lower level legal and judicial systems in their districts (or counties).

The governments of states (or provinces) are organized and function much like nation-states, except that they are limited to service roles subordinate to the nation-states. The major difference in services is that nation-states retain control of relationships with other nation-states, and over laws necessary to relationships between the provinces or states and the well-being of the entire nation-state.

IMPROVEMENT OF STATE (PROVINCE) BOUNDARIES

There may be great differences in the sizes and populations of states and provinces, which are the subdivisions of nation-states. In the United States, some of the small states came into being in the early years of United States history. Some of the larger ones came into existence many years later. Often state sizes and boundaries were set before there was any valid estimate of the future economy and population growth of the states created.

In every case, boundaries were determined primarily by politics, the early states being the result of British colonial policies. Later ones came about through expansion of United States jurisdiction, with a number of those in the first half of the 1800s being the result of political maneuvering prior to the Civil War between the states over the issues of slavery and the extent of "states' rights".

A major result of the present state boundaries is unequal representation in the United States Senate, where every state has two senators. At the same time states containing large populations, although having only two senators, are cultivated carefully by both major political parties for two reasons. First, gaining the numerous electoral votes in the states with large populations can be critical to winning the presidency. Second, gaining the majority of the seats in the United States House of Representatives depends largely on winning congressional district representative elections in the states with large populations.

The congressional representative districts are based on a population size standard, with the result that any necessary redrawing of congressional district boundaries by the State Legislatures can involve much political maneuvering. In some instances, the redrawing of the district boundaries is followed by judicial court battles, as occurred recently in Texas. (The goal should be representational equity, and such re-districting should be accomplished within two years following the United States decennial census determination of the state's population).

Improvement of the boundaries of states would help to improve the national political process, as well as representative democracy for the citizens of the United States. State boundaries could be improved to better recognize physical geography and unity in economic and social interests in the different parts of the nation. The southwestern part of the State of Washington adjacent to the Columbia River is better related through physical geography and economic interests to the State of Oregon, than it is to the remainder of the State of Washington. Similarly, a far eastern portion of the State of Oregon would relate better to the southern portion of the State of Idaho. Another example is the panhandle area of the State of Nebraska; most of that area would relate better to the State of Wyoming to the west. In turn, that part of western Iowa near the Missouri River would relate better to eastern Nebraska than to the remainder of Iowa.

States or provinces should be delineated by more effective boundaries. The size and number of the states or provinces should depend on the geographic size of the nation state, other geographical factors, and the density of population.

It would be possible to redraw the state boundaries in the continental United States and have approximately the same number of states, but with more similarity in population size and geographic area. Any losses in so-called "political clout" at the national level, which would result from boundary improvement, would be more than compensated for by economic benefits to residents of the states, as well as increased governmental efficiency and lowered cost to taxpayers.

In states or provinces, the location of the headquarters for management of governmental services should be in a city of medium to large size. Central location geographically within the state or province can be advantageous, but is not essential. Relationship to the geographic areas and populations to be served is far more significant.

NATION-STATE GOVERNMENTS

The governments of nation-states, like all other human organizations, include policy making; record keeping; research, analysis and legal counsel; financial and support services; and operations. In the United States, the elected members of the United States Senate and House of Representatives are policy makers. The President is the elected chief executive and also a policy maker. In many other nation states the King or President is more of a social function head, while the leader of the elected majority in the Parliament is the Prime Minister, the chief executive.

The physical security of citizens and their possessions is, as it should be, the primary goal in the enactment of laws and the formulation of administrative regulations to carry out the laws. Police functions, a department of legal prosecutors, an independent court system, and correctional institutions are essential to such security.

Research (including the gathering of intelligence) and analysis are basic to governmental functions. Legal counsel is essential in all governmental operations and support activities.

Once policy makers determine a budget for governmental services, arranging for financing and accounting for expenditures for governmental services is the function of a finance or treasury department. This department should also control the minting and printing of money for use in commercial exchange. In the United States, a Comptroller General, appointed for an 11-year term in office, heads an organization for fiscal auditing and maintaining financial records. The Library of Congress also maintains governmental records.

Governmental operations include both support for and legal regulation of financial services, commerce, health services, social services, education, historical preservation, construction, transportation, communication, resource development and conservation, agriculture, and industrial production.

Nation-states also conduct a broad range of relationships with other nation-states in commerce and travel through a foreign relations department and other departments. A border patrol, coast guard, and customs service are a necessary part of such operations. As would be expected in light of the competition, and at times in our era open conflict between nation-states, there is a defense department including land, sea, and air armed forces.

IMPROVEMENT OF NATION-STATE BOUNDARIES

Nation-states exercise great influence over the population within their jurisdictions. Consequently, leaders of nation-states and their advisors have considered the boundaries of nation-states of critical importance. Leaders have tried, not always successfully, to locate boundaries to include all their particular social or interest groups within the nation-state's area. This usually has meant all those people of the same ethnicity: i.e. language, religion, race, and cultural characteristics. Political leaders and commercial/industrial interests have also tried to locate the boundaries of their nation-states, to include what they currently consider more militarily defensible features and greater economic power.

The result is that the Earth is divided into nation-states delineated by boundaries that in some areas are logical, but in other areas came about through political maneuvers and open conflicts in the past. Some of these are not effective boundaries and can only lead to continued nation-state conflict. Examples of poor nation-state boundaries are especially evident in Africa and Asia, where the European colonial powers drew boundaries and divided areas with little regard for either the ethnicity of people or natural geographical boundaries. Iraq is an example of a nation-state with boundaries drawn by outsiders.

In the future nation-states should be defined by boundaries based upon geographical factors that argue for national unity. Such factors include a specific and recognizable segment of the Earth's surface, its human population, and areas meeting their commercial, industrial, agricultural, and social services' needs. The goals of nation-state boundaries should be governments with less internal conflict and sound economies.

Previous history cannot be ignored, but commonality of economic and social interests surely should take precedence over political power and its interests. Maintaining the boundaries of a realm created originally by outside political and military power, as was often done in the era of colonialism, should not be considered primary in importance.

Obviously, the historical influences and significance of language, religion, and other cultural influences are important. However, racial discrimination should be discouraged and should not be a factor in delineating effective boundaries. Willingness to learn about, understand, and tolerate the religious faiths of others could minimize conflicts within and between nation-states. Bigotry in any form is certain to lead to conflict.

To avoid social conflict some, but not all, differences in cultural characteristics and social attitudes should be met with tolerance. However, there should be clear and strong recognition that language is humankind's greatest tool. A nation-state must rely on the use in public of one language if it is to be successful in providing stable government, a sound economy, and continued peaceful intercourse among the citizens of the nation state.

BOUNDARIES FOR THE EUROPEAN UNION

The recently created European Union can serve as an example for the improvement of nation-state boundaries. The European Union covers a segment of the Earth's surface that, if not expanded too far to the east in Eurasia, surely can provide commonality in economic interests. The area's long history of internal conflicts argues strongly for one political unit, in order to gain the peace and economic stability so desired by and for the people of Europe.

There are two major challenges to gaining real unity for the European Union. The first is the remnants of long-established competing political and special economic interest powers in the separate realms of Europe. The second is a still-needed decision on a single governmental language, to minimize internal misunderstandings, and to promote economic unity of the European Union. This latter could be the more serious of the two challenges.

At present, race and religion are lesser challenges within the European Union, but these may loom larger with migration from other areas of the Earth, unless actions are taken to oppose any actions leading to misunderstandings, intolerance, and social conflict. Finally, the capitol of a nation-state such as a united Europe would best be located in a large city in a relatively central location as to geography, economy, and population of a well-defined European Union.

IMPORTANCE OF BOUNDARIES

Well-located boundaries of nation-states, provinces (or states), districts (or counties), and municipal governments (settlements) can enhance the economic, security, and social needs of people living within the areas enclosed. Such boundaries avoid mistaken inclusions or exclusions of areas, as well as a lowered level of commonality of interests. Well-located boundaries can lead to better decisions regarding use of natural resources, industrial production, commercial services, and the location of transportation routes and their capacities for service.

BOUNDARIES AND TRANSPORTATION ROUTES

Inter-city transportation routes differ from the intra-city routes within municipalities discussed earlier. Inter-city routes should not be located to provide boundaries but rather as a network of connections between settlements within higher governmental jurisdictions. Lack of a complete network of connections results in a lowered level of service for some settlements and for some segments of a district or province.

Despite the increased importance of air travel and transport in recent times, surface transportation facilities remain essential. However, truck and bus service has for a long time over-shadowed rail travel and transport between settlements in the United States. Reliance on large truck and bus service has increased construction and maintenance costs for highways and freeways between settlements.

Recently there has been some effort to increase rail travel and transport. However, hasty decisions to renew use of existing rail lines should be avoided. Expanded rail use should be carefully planned to provide an appropriate network of rail connections between settlements, while avoiding some of the errors of the past.

EXISTING RAILROAD LINES

Examination of an early 20th century atlas will reveal a rather astonishing array of routes selected and railroad lines constructed in the era of great extension of railroads in the United States. This occurred under the unregulated competition between the railroad companies permitted at the time. Railroad companies sometimes selected routes as devices for competition with other companies, rather than to meet real service needs. The result was increased growth, or even the creation of settlements, where such settlement growth was unnecessary to serve adjoining rural areas. Growth also occurred at crew change and engine service locations on the railroad lines. At the same time, railroad companies ignored or underserved some settlements and their rural service areas.

HIGHWAYS AND FREEWAYS

In the United States, transportation planners of inter-city highway and freeway routes have carelessly by-passed smaller settlements, locating routes through less productive land areas in order to expedite service between large settlements with greater political influence. The result has been the creation of secondary commercial centers in smaller settlements, or even the creation of new commercial centers and settlements in what may be less advantageous locations.

Inter-city transport and travel routes, both highway and railroad, should be located to lead to, but not through, the principal commercial centers of settlements. Passage directly through the commercial center of a settlement can be a disruptive influence. Care should be taken to provide connection to an intra-city route (an important arterial street, perhaps carrying public transit) providing good access to and from the principal commercial center of a settlement. Necessary at the same time are zoning regulations to carry out appropriate land-use planning.

Care has not always been exercised to provide efficient intra-city arterial routes, because government often neglects its own land use planning and zoning regulations. One Oregon town is an example. US Highway 99 E passed the east side of Woodburn. Instead of leading to more growth in the town's original commercial center, a business ribbon was allowed to grow along Highway 99 E and erode its value as an inter-city transport route. Later, Interstate 5 passed the west side of the town. Today, business activity continues to grow both along 99E and near the on and off ramps of the Interstate 5 interchange. The old commercial center of the town has been neglected, and the center has decayed.

ROUTES TOO CLOSE TO CITY CENTERS

Perhaps more troublesome, in some large cities inter-city transportation routes (railroad and highway) have been located so close to the principal commercial center as to create barriers both to intra-city traffic movement and to future desirable expansion of the center. In Portland, Oregon, Highway 99 W once passed directly between the principal commercial center, located on the west side of the Willamette River, and the river itself. A waterfront park replaced Highway 99 W.

The present route of Interstate 5 is immediately adjacent to the east side of the Willamette River. At that location not only numerous ramps to and from bridges crossing the river to the principal commercial center on the west side of the river were needed, but possible desirable expansion of the principal commercial center to the east side of the river was prevented. The result has been to force east-side extension of the principal commercial center of Portland to a location to the north and east of Interstate 5 (the Lloyd Center area).

In recent years, discussion in Portland has centered on relocating Interstate 5 further to the east, away from the Willamette River, but the cost of relocation has been and will be a deterrent for an unforeseeable length of time. The question of relocation is also clouded by the fact that a north-south railroad line, passing through Portland, is immediately east of the present Interstate 5 location.

OTHER ROUTE IMPACTS IN CITIES

In large cities, failure to coordinate transportation planning and land use planning has had an adverse impact on residential neighborhoods (elementary school areas), especially those near the city centers. The alignments of additional intra-city auto and transit routes, and sometimes inter-city freeway routes, have segmented neighborhoods. Newer and seemingly improved routes have been developed to support or replace older ones, instead of first selecting an optimum route (or routes) and then increasing capacity or effectiveness along the same alignment over time. In numerous cases, new route alignments have stimulated the growth of new commercial centers and "business ribbons", while older commercial centers declined in value and appearance.

Development of one-way couplets for short distances along existing arterials is an effective and less costly way of increasing arterial capacity and encouraging business center growth at planned locations, instead of allowing more "business ribbon" growth.

Most significant, the result of segmenting residential areas with additional arterial routes has been erosion of the quality of environment in residential neighborhoods. This in turn has led to continued flight of families with children to outlying city locations, and a continued need for re-examination of school enrollments, both in the close-in areas and in the outlying areas of cities.

To minimize the problem, there is a need to increase coordination of decisions regarding major arterial streets and transit lines with land use planning and zoning, in order to protect neighborhoods (elementary school areas) and communities (high school areas), and to support well-located commercial centers to serve such residential areas. Such coordination is also advantageous in the planning for neighborhood and community playground and park facilities.

Basic to the planning described above is planning the location of boundaries for residential neighborhoods and communities served by elementary schools and high schools and by related playground and park facilities. Such planning for boundaries can make for more livable cities. Stable boundaries are essential to long-term livability of residential areas.

ESTABLISHING BOUNDARIES FOR GOVERNMENTAL JURISDICTIONS

Regarding boundaries for municipalities (settlements) and higher governmental jurisdictions, a need exists for guidelines for improving such boundaries. Settling on guidelines for establishing good boundaries, to avoid the problems discussed earlier, requires recalling the considerations involved in the establishment of settlements as humans migrated and occupied most of the Earth. Those were the availability of food and water, effective travel and transport routes, and security. Organization and leadership were essential in the development of each settlement. As settlements grew and the provision of security advanced, humans began to live in rural areas beyond settlement boundaries, and to increase the development of food and other resources. Commercial services grew in size to meet the needs not only of the residents of settlements, but also of those living in rural areas. Routes and means of travel and transportation grew in economic importance.

History reveals the steady advance of technology and the growth of human populations; however, the basic needs of humans in both settlements and rural areas remain the same. The boundaries of settlements and higher governmental jurisdictions should be well drawn to serve the residents of both urban and rural areas. Boundaries should encompass populations of similar economic, social, and security interests, and should minimize human conflict.

Boundaries based on the significant physical features of our Earth are more desirable than politically constructed boundaries. Oceans, seas, gulfs, large bays, and large lakes are obstacles to ease of transportation and communication, but they do provide desirable boundaries. In some instances, this is true also of small bays, inlets, and lakes. However, care must be exercised in locating boundaries within or across the smaller bodies of water; these may be unifiers of commercial and social activities, rather than dividers.

BOUNDARIES ON LAND

Delineation of effective boundaries on land areas ought to consider various factors that are recognizable and identifiable. Mountains, hills, plains, islands, peninsulas and headlands, and stream drainage areas provide recognizable boundaries. Soil types, abundant water or shortage of water; natural vegetation; populations of land animals; and sea, lake, and stream life provide identifiable evidence for effective boundary establishment.

Additionally, differences in temperatures and climates occur as one moves from the equatorial areas to the polar areas of the Earth. Different wind systems and ocean currents affect climate. Difference in temperatures and climate in continental land areas is due to isolation by mountains or distance from the moderating influences of oceans and seas.

Land elevations ought to be a basic consideration. Land elevations separating water drainage areas are desirable locations for boundaries. An example is the principal range of the Alps Mountains in Europe. However, much can depend on the width of the mountain area and the lower elevations adjoining the mountain chain. For example, much of the length of the Rocky Mountains chain in the United States is more of a unifier than a boundary for some of the western American states, because of the dryer climate areas existing beyond both sides of the mountain chain. More logical boundary locations east of the chain are where there is a transition from the dryer high plains adjoining the mountain chain to the lower well-watered plains farther east. West of the Rocky Mountain chain boundary lines between the mountain area states and Pacific Coast area states ought to be based on the physical terrain of the Great Basin area to the west and present land development patterns.

In addition, there may be instances where the headwaters of a stream may be isolated on that side of the crest line of a mountain range opposite from the stream's lower course drainage area. This can either be the result of the headwater's erosion back through the crest of the range, or because the stream existed before the mountain range rose. The side of the mountain range to which the isolated headwater area best relates, and the most desirable boundary location, depends on the area's size and physical boundaries.

In more level land areas, the somewhat higher elevations between river and stream courses are more desirable locations for boundaries than the streams themselves. Most rivers and streams are unifiers rather than dividers of agricultural, commercial, and social activities. There are some exceptions; one may be a stream flowing through a deep canyon or through an arid area containing no development along the stream. A stream in a swampy area, where no development exists along the stream, may be another. However, possible exceptions to the general rule require careful evaluation.

BOUNDARIES CROSSING STREAMS

Often boundaries must cross streams. A suitable location for crossing is where there is change in climate, natural vegetation, soils, and agricultural characteristics between an upper portion and a lower portion of a stream drainage area. The transition in the plains east of the Rocky Mountains provides examples for this.

A more desirable boundary would either cross the upper branches of a stream at a location a reasonable distance above where stream branches join, or cross at a desirable location below where the branches join. These locations would avoid isolating small areas of land and their residents between either a junction of two stream branches, or between a stream and a stream branch lower down the main stream drainage area.

Boundaries would best cross at right angles to the main direction of the stream's flow. However, a stream can itself be an acceptable boundary where, for a very limited distance, it is flowing approximately at right angles to the general direction of the stream's flow, and a bridge does not cross it; then a stream can serve as an economic and social divider rather than a unifier.

Boundary locations need to recognize existing villages, towns or cities, and the rural areas to which each provides commercial and social services. Generally, settlements develop and grow at locations based on geographic and economic factors, and a variety of human decisions regarding the services the settlement can provide to its residents and those in its rural service area.

However, the choice of a transportation route alignment, and this may have been arbitrary, may have influenced site selection and growth of a settlement. An example is the location of the town of Julesburg, Colorado. The first and possibly the best geographic location of a Julesburg settlement was on Lodgepole Creek, which flows into the South Platte River just east of Ovid, Colorado. The second location, long ago abandoned, was several miles northeast of Ovid on the Union Pacific railroad line, built in the 1860s. The third and current location of Julesburg is several miles to the southeast of the second location, where a Union Pacific railroad line extending to Denver, Colorado, joined the older Union Pacific line. That settlement and its rural service area have grown and must be recognized now.

BOUNDARY LOCATIONS ON TRANSPORTATION ROUTES

Access roads or streets, highways (whether limited access or not), railroad lines, or canals do not provide satisfactory boundaries for governmental jurisdictions. These routes serve governmental jurisdictions rather than serving as boundaries. Their use as boundaries creates problems as to maintenance responsibility and police jurisdiction. Desirable locations for jurisdictional boundaries are the rear property lines of properties fronting on a local road or street. When a jurisdictional boundary crosses a road, street, or other route, it should cross as nearly as possible at right angles and then follow side boundary lines between property ownerships.

GUIDELINES FOR BOUNDARY LOCATIONS

The following are recommended for use as guidelines in delineating boundaries between governmental jurisdictions in order to enhance unity and efficiency for them:

1. The Earth's surface consists of specific and recognizable segments: the Earth's land elevations, different climate areas, water bodies of size and significance, stream drainage areas, and stream courses.
2. With few exceptions, the most productive agricultural lands and the most advantageous sites for settlements are located along stream courses.
3. Human populations wish to occupy land areas that best meet their commercial, agricultural, industrial, social service, and public security needs.
4. Settlements serve adjoining service areas and boundary lines should be located with consideration of those service areas.
5. The most efficient and least disruptive transportation systems and routes are those that provide a service web between but not through settlements.
6. Significant language, historical, religious, and cultural factors.
7. The need for peaceful relationships between human populations and between the governments representing people.
8. The need for limitation of population growth to ensure adequate quantities of water and agricultural land to sustain human livability, and avoid the conflicts certain to arise with shortages in these resources.

Such guidelines could be used to improve boundaries for states (provinces), counties (districts), and settlements in the United States, and boundaries in other nation-states as well. At the international level, some of the most stubborn and threatening disputes and conflicts between nation-states could also be resolved through application of these boundary guidelines. Humans on the five major continents surely would benefit from efforts to improve nation-state boundaries and minimize boundary disputes, bitter conflicts, and open warfare that now contribute to human tragedy, misery, and economic loss.

DDC

THE POSSIBILITY OF CYCLES

AN ESSAY
BY DALE D CANNADY

Since ancient times, humans have been captivated by the supernatural, any perceived possible influence upon events beyond the comprehension of the five human senses. Desiring to understand the causes of strange or incomprehensible occurrences, individuals and groups have expressed concern and speculation as to the source of such occurrences. Early in human history, efforts were made to explain such events through mythological narratives about the activities of supernatural gods and goddesses. Warnings of future occurrences, based upon mythological understandings, led ultimately to a belief in omens, intuitions, and divinations, such as those given by the Oracle of Delphi in Ancient Greece.

Although mythology, stargazing, astrology, religion, and ultimately science have each attempted to explain the incomprehensible, humans often continue to be drawn to supernatural explanation. Thought has continued to center on a hypothesis that life is influenced by supernatural, cyclical impacts. The purpose of this essay is to examine the development of this hypothesis, and to test its application on one facet of American political history: United States presidencies.

EARLY STARGAZERS

Perhaps 6000 to 7000 years ago, stargazers, in response to speculation regarding cyclical seasonal changes on Earth that affect human lives, began carefully observing all parts of the Universe visible at night to the naked eye. They observed that the Moon moved regularly across the starry background visible from Earth at night. They surmised that the Moon revolved in a pre-ordained course around the Earth. They observed also that the view of the starry background visible at Sun's dawn and dusk slowly changed. They mistakenly decided that the Sun also revolved around Earth, but at a much slower pace than the Moon did.

ASTROLOGY

Early stargazers gradually developed a hypothesis, now known as Astrology. They determined that the starry background visible from Earth in the night sky could be divided into 12 recognizable segments. Small variations exist in the width of the 12 segments. The 12 segments were seen from year to year in a cyclical pattern. Astrologers gave names to the 12 segments of the sky (the astrological Zodiac) to assist in communicating their hypothetical understandings to their peers.

Astrologers observed that the 12 segments of the sky related cyclically to the four seasons of the year. The belief continued that both the Moon and the Sun revolved around the Earth. Early stargazers also found the five planets nearest to Earth (Mercury, Venus, Mars, Jupiter, and Saturn) and noted that they were unlike the apparently fixed stars. These planets were seen to be moving at different but constant speeds across the starry background. In time it was decided that each of the planets moved in a cyclical pattern.

Given their powerful belief in a supernatural world, astrologers concluded that the cyclical locations of the Sun, Moon, and the five planets within the 12 segments of the sky must influence events on Earth. They developed horoscopes, displaying the current locations of the Moon, Sun, and the planets, to attribute influences on peoples' personal characteristics and personalities -- and on current events.

In addition to the five planets located by early stargazers, contemporary astrologers create horoscopes based on inclusion of the planets Uranus, Neptune, and Pluto, discovered and visible since the telescope was developed. Scientists have recently decided that Pluto is a planetoid or asteroid and not a planet. Whether astrologers will adjust their horoscopes to recognize this new knowledge remains to be seen.

Eventually astrologers began to concentrate on forecasting the future, even making forecasts for each day of the week. This detailed forecasting of the future finally led to total rejection of astrology by scientists at the beginning of the 19th century.

THE DEVELOPMENT OF SCIENCE

Science is the quest for verifiable knowledge. The early stargazers have been replaced by astronomers, whose advancing technology has made possible the verification of some of the supernatural. Scientists have ascertained that the Moon orbits Earth, that Earth is a planet orbiting the Sun, and that each of the other seven planets also orbit the Sun. We know that the cyclical ebb and flow of the tides in Earth's oceans are caused by the gravitational influence of the Moon on the Earth. We know that Earth revolves once each day in a predictable cycle, as it orbits the Sun once each year. We know that the cyclical seasons of our planet's year result from Earth's 23.5 degree tilt in its annual orbit around the Sun. Although essential to life on Earth, our Sun is now known to be only an average-sized star located within an arm of the Milky Way galaxy, only one of an immense number of galaxies in the Universe beyond our Solar system.

The physical impact and cyclical influence of the Sun on Earth is now also well recognized. Scientists have demonstrated that the Earth is a target for radiation from the Milky Way and the Universe beyond. Scientific efforts are ongoing, and more knowledge will be gained in the future, concerning impacts on the Earth not only from the Sun, but also from the Milky Way and the immense number of more distant galaxies in the ever-changing Universe. Knowing that the Sun and Moon maintain cyclical influences on the Earth (including sun spot activity), it seems reasonable to continue to consider the possibility of cyclical influences on Earth and its inhabitants from the Milky Way and the Universe beyond.

POSSIBILITY OF CYCLICAL IMPACTS

One avenue for exploration is for persons interested in the events of history, pre-history, and Earth history to look for clues that would indicate cyclical influence in events on Earth. Indications of cyclical activity may appear to be contradicted by inconsistencies or irregularities in time, but irregularities may be an inherent aspect of cycles that research and evaluation may uncover. Earth is a small planet in our Solar system, and far less than a speck in the Universe, about whose size and impacts scientists have almost everything to learn.

The possibility of cycles is evaluated herein through an examination of historical events. Review of American political history suggests that cyclical influences are at work. It is logical to speculate that the causes are universal forces located in space beyond Earth, and that their influences are part of a natural cycle of human events.

AMERICAN PRESIDENTIAL HISTORY

A cursory review of American presidential history suggests that universal influences may be at work. For example, some historians see parallels between President Abraham Lincoln, President John Kennedy, and their secretaries, named Kennedy and Lincoln. A list of parallels between the two presidents was published after Kennedy's assassination. They included comparisons of the assassins John Wilkes Booth and Lee Harvey Oswald.

Also of interest is the curse placed upon General William Henry Harrison by the Native American shaman, called The Prophet. Harrison had defeated a coalition of Native Americans, led temporarily by the Prophet (brother of the great chief Tecumseh), in the Battle of Tippecanoe in Indiana. This renowned victory contributed to Harrison being elected United States president in 1840. He died one month following his inauguration in 1841. Subsequently, presidents elected at 20-year intervals died or were assassinated while in office. This led to speculation that Harrison's demise, and the deaths at 20-year intervals of future presidents, might be the cyclical result of the Prophet's curse.

A time disruption in this death cycle occurred when Franklin Roosevelt was elected president in 1940. Roosevelt did not die until 1945, after serving a third term and beginning a fourth term as president. However, Wendell Wilkie, the losing candidate in the 1940 election, died in 1944. Clearly the imminence of WWII influenced American voters to elect Roosevelt to a third term in office, despite the traditional two-term limit.

The cycle of deaths of presidents elected at 20-year intervals remained unbroken until President Ronald Reagan, elected in 1980, barely survived an assassination attempt in 1981. In September 2011 the fourth airliner of the four seized by El-Qaeda terrorists for the attacks on the United States is thought to have been destined to strike the White House, the home of the United States president. Were these events, at roughly 20-year intervals mere coincidence, or did the Prophet, Tecumseh's brother, initiate a supernatural cycle at the time he rendered the curse?

These parallels among previous presidents of the United States arouse interest in the possibility of universal cycles. The presidents are individuals of great influence. Research on two groups of people close to the presidents, the presidents' wives and the vice presidents, might also be supportive of cyclical impact on the United States presidency.

100-YEAR TIME SEGMENTS

Review of presidential history suggests that it consists of approximate 100-year time segments that may reflect universal cyclical impacts, with minor variations in the timing of those impacts. Presidencies are by their constitutional nature cyclical, and this may account for some variation. Nonetheless, it may be reasonable to surmise that cyclical impacts at century intervals result from forces in the Universe beyond our Sun, including variations in those forces. With this in mind, the following is a limited examination of presidential history, intended to examine the possibility of cyclical impacts on events here on Earth.

INITIATORS OF CHANGE
AT CENTURY INTERVALS

The United States has been served by especially able leaders, beginning with the first years of American independence, and continuing at century intervals to the present. Those leaders were George Washington, revered as the father of his country, in the 1780s; Presidents James Garfield, Chester Arthur, and Grover Cleveland (the first term) in the 1880s; and President Ronald Reagan in the 1980s.

THE 1780S

The American War for Independence from the British Empire ended with the American victory at Yorktown, Virginia, in 1781 and the peace treaty of 1783. However, during the 1780s it became evident that the Articles of Confederation governing the thirteen former British colonies were ineffective.

George Washington, the military hero of America's War for Independence, became involved in the movement leading to a Constitutional Convention. He served as chairman of the convention, and must have influenced the content and the adoption of the United States Constitution.

The United States Constitution was adopted in 1787, and the first government elected under it began operation in 1789. Adoption and activation of the Constitution was of critical importance to the success of democratic government in the United States, becoming a precedent for constitutional democracy elsewhere in the world. Washington's able political leadership in the 1780s may represent initiation of a cycle of change that will continue to influence presidential history.

THE 1880S

In 1881, a century after Yorktown, an initiator of change emerged once again. James Garfield of Ohio became the 20th president of the United States (1881-). In the presidential election of 1880, Garfield defeated the Democratic Party nominee, former Union Army General Winfield Scott Hancock, a native of Pennsylvania. Garfield was nominated at the Republican Party convention in 1880, following a struggle between supporters of James Blaine of Maine and the "Stalwarts" who supported another term for President Ulysses Grant. Grant, the military hero of the American Civil War, had already served two terms as president (1869 - 1873 and 1873 - 1877), his presidency marred by corruption.

After Levi Morton of New York declined the Republican Party nomination for vice-president in 1880, Chester Arthur of New York (a native of Vermont) was nominated. This was a concession to US Senator Roscoe Conkling of New York, a leader of the "Stalwarts".

At the time Garfield became president, appointments to Federal governmental positions were made under the "spoils system", initiated by President Andrew Jackson. In appointing the Collector of Customs in New York City, President Garfield encountered the opposition of US Senators Roscoe Conkling and Thomas Platt of New York. Garfield pushed strongly for approval of his nominee for the position. The two senators from New York resigned from the US Senate in protest of Garfield's action.

In July 1881, President Garfield was shot by a disappointed office-seeker, who shouted that he was a "Stalwart" and wanted Arthur to be president. Garfield was disabled but lived for 80 days. Upon Garfield's death, Chester Arthur became the 21st president (1881 - 1885).

As vice-president, Arthur had not supported Garfield in the dispute with Senator Roscoe Conkling. As president, Arthur's thinking evolved, and he advanced Garfield's aims and plans. Then Arthur supported the Pendleton Act, a first step in creating the federal civil service to replace the "spoils system". This was a major step forward in American government, a result of Arthur's able leadership and initiative.

Unfortunately, Arthur's service as president was not rewarded. Although he allowed his name to be submitted for nomination, he was defeated on the fourth ballot at the Republican Party convention in 1884, probably due to his advanced thinking and actions.

Although Arthur was a close friend of Roscoe Conkling of New York (long an enemy of James Blaine of Maine), Arthur supported Blaine at the Republican Party convention in 1884. Blaine received the Republican nomination, but was defeated in the presidential election by the Democratic Party nominee (Stephen) Grover Cleveland of New York.

Grover Cleveland was born in New Jersey, reared in Upper New York, and lived in Western New York. Cleveland's first term as president (1885 - 1889) followed his defeat of the Republican nominee, James Blaine of Maine. Grover Cleveland was the first Democratic Party president elected in the 24 years since Abraham Lincoln became president in 1861, just before the American Civil War began. As president, Cleveland fought unsuccessfully in behalf of American farmers to reduce high protective tariffs installed over the years by the Republicans. Thus, Grover Cleveland initiated the liberal political movements of the 1890s and early 1900s that arose in opposition to the wave of conservatism that followed the Civil War.

Cleveland's vice-president (1885 -) was Thomas Hendricks of Indiana, a native of Ohio. Hendricks had sought the Democratic Party presidential nomination several times. He had been the nominee for vice-president with Democrat presidential nominee Samuel Tilden of New York, who was defeated in the election of 1876. Hendricks was again nominated for vice-president in 1884. Vice-President Hendricks died in office in November 1885.

THE 1980S

In 1981, two centuries after Yorktown, another initiator of change, Ronald Reagan of California (a native of Illinois) became the 40th president (1981 - 1985 and 1985 -1989). In 1981, a century after Garfield's assassination, Ronald Reagan was fortunate and barely survived an assassination attempt.

Nominated at the Republican Party Convention in 1980, Reagan had defeated the bid of President Jimmy Carter of Georgia for re-election. In 1984 Reagan again gained the Republican Party nomination. In that election he defeated the Democratic Party nominee, Walter Mondale of Minnesota, who had been vice-president during Carter's term as president. The vice-president in both of Ronald Reagan's terms as president (1981 - 1985 and 1985 - 1989) was George H. W. Bush of Texas (a native of Connecticut).

In the 1980s President Reagan initiated a long-term movement by the Republican Party toward move conservative government in the United States. Strongly conservative, Reagan opposed what he termed "big government", and his tax and economic policies came to be known as "trickle -down economics". In Reagan's first term as president, a short lived economic recession followed the inflationary spiral that began during Jimmy Carter's presidency, but the economy recovered quickly.

One of President Reagan's aims was to initiate change in the relationship between the United States and the Communist world. He put pressure on the Communist Soviet Union, which he called "The Evil Empire", by refusing to discuss armament reduction with a sequence of three Soviet Union leaders. Instead, Reagan initiated a program of US armament expansion and actively supported the opponents of expanded Communist rule in Afghanistan, the Contra opposition to the leftist Ortega regime in Nicaragua, and the Solidarity Movement in Communist Poland.

The expenditure for arms, the rapid growth of the national debt, and fear of nuclear war brought increased concern and active opposition within the United States. The sale of arms to Iran, and the secret transfer of funds to the Contras in Nicaragua, proved embarrassing to President Reagan, once they became known.

However, as president, Reagan did turn the tide in the Cold War struggle to halt the expansion of Russian Communism. The result was the end of Communist rule during 1989 - 1991, not only in Central Europe, but also in Russia itself. The end of the Cold War with Russia was helped by armament discussions, and the reform efforts of Michael Gorbachev, the last Communist leader of Russia. The termination of Communist rule of Russia was gained by the people of Russia with the courageous leadership of Boris Yeltsin in 1991.

CYCLICAL PARALLELS

Interesting parallels exist among Washington, Garfield, Arthur, and Reagan. Washington was viewed by his peers as a sober, strong, and persuasive leader. The United States Constitution, developed and adopted under his chairmanship, has been influential in many other nations. Garfield evidently was an able and eloquent leader. He rose to Major General in the Union Army in the American Civil War, had long experience in the US House of Representatives, and might have been a far more influential president had he lived. The fathers of both Washington and Garfield died when their sons were young.

Earlier in life Arthur gained a reputation as an able administrator; as president he demonstrated a capacity to change his political views and pursue higher goals. Earlier in his life Ronald Reagan believed in Franklin Roosevelt's New Deal. Later, he became the leader of the Screen Actors Guild, a union, but as a result of Communist activities on the part of a few individuals within the film industry, he became a Republican whose strong conservative views have had lasting influence on our time. Reagan has been recognized as very personable, persuasive, and capable of strongly pursuing key goals, as were Washington, Garfield, and Arthur.

Washington, Arthur, and Reagan all were over six feet in height. Both Washington and Reagan were very popular presidents. Both enjoyed rural life and riding horses. Reagan's death in 2004, after a long illness, brought a sense of national loss resembling that which followed George Washington's death in 1799.

Grover Cleveland was a strong and determined leader, who faced stiff conservative opposition in the US Congress during his first term as president. He became president a second time in 1893. He was the only Democrat to serve as president between 1861 and 1913 and was a forerunner of more liberal actions by later presidents.

EXPANSIONIST LEADERS
AT CENTURY INTERVALS

Three presidents promoted significant extension of America's prestige and power in the world at 100 year intervals: George Washington, Benjamin Harrison, and George H. W. Bush. Washington, the first president elected under the newly adopted United States Constitution, began his first term as president a century ahead of Harrison and two centuries ahead of the senior George Bush.

1789

In 1788 General George Washington of Virginia was the obvious choice to become the first president of the United States, under the newly adopted Constitution. He won the electoral vote in the 1788 election. As president, Washington's efforts were directed toward security of the new nation and expansion of the land area controlled by the United States.

John Adams of Massachusetts was second in the electoral vote, and under the Constitutional provision effective at that time he became vice-president. Adams had been one of the key members of the Continental Congress during the American Revolution and had served as an American representative in both France and England.

Re-elected again in 1792, Washington and Adams served two terms as president and vice-president (1789 - 1793 and 1793 - 1797). George Clinton, a powerful politician and longtime Governor of New York, later a Democratic Republican, was third in electoral votes in 1792.

1889

A century later in 1888, the Republican nominee for president was Benjamin Harrison of Indiana (grandson of William Henry Harrison, the 9th president). Harrison defeated the bid of Democrat Grover Cleveland for re-election, and became the 23rd president (1889 - 1893). Cleveland won the popular vote, but lost the electoral vote to Harrison.

In Harrison's administration the United States participated in the first meeting of the Organization of American States and became active in helping to resolve disagreements between nations.

Levi Morton, a native of Vermont, served as Harrison's vice president (1889 - 1893). Morton had been in business in New Hampshire and Massachusetts, and in banking in New York. He had been active in Republican Party politics as well as serving as United States minister to France.

1989

In 1988 George H. W. Bush of Texas, who had been Ronald Reagan's vice-president (1981 - 1989), gained the Republican Party nomination and defeated the Democrat nominee Michael Dukakis. Dukakis, like John Adams two centuries earlier, was from Massachusetts.

George H. W. Bush was the 41st president (1989 - 1993). Dan Quayle of Indiana, who had been in the newspaper business, as well as active in Republican politics, served as Bush's vice-president (1989 - 1993).

The wall between communist East Germany and democratic West Germany came down in 1989. The Gulf War in 1992, initiated and led by the United States, resulted in the defeat of Saddam Hussein's Iraq. Iraq had invaded and seized Kuwait, which had been separated from Iraq by Great Britain, following the dismemberment of the Ottoman Empire at the end of World War I.

CYCLICAL PARALLELS

Biographies of George Washington, Benjamin Harrison, and George H. W. Bush, who became presidents at century intervals, also reveal parallels. Each of them gained recognition in military roles earlier in life. Washington's first military experiences were in the British/American Colonists campaign to drive the French out of the area west of the Appalachian Mountains, during the French and Indian Wars. Later, Washington led the army of the American colonies in the American War for Independence. Benjamin Harrison formed an Indiana regiment, and rose to Brigadier General in the Atlanta campaign during the American Civil War. George H. W. Bush first gained recognition as the youngest US Navy aviator in World War II.

As a young man, Washington surveyed land in western Virginia. Later, he owned land in the Ohio River area. As a young man, Harrison moved west from Ohio to Indiana to practice law. George H. W. Bush moved from Connecticut to Texas after World War II, and gained success in the oil business before entering politics.

The terms in office of these three presidents can be termed successful; significant expansion of United States leadership and power occurred under each of them. In his first term as president, Washington used the Jay Treaty with Great Britain to gain American control over the old "Northwest Territory". He also gained commercial access to the Mississippi River and New Orleans. A century later in Harrison's presidency, the present northwestern states (South Dakota, North Dakota, Montana, Wyoming, Idaho, and Washington) were admitted to the Union. During Harrison's presidency the United States for the first time exercised leadership among the nations of North and South America. George H. W. Bush's presidency witnessed the fall of the Communist Empire in Central Europe in 1989 and in Russia in 1991. The rapid and successful coalition of nations under American leadership resulted in the defeat of Iraq in 1992 in the Gulf War. These expansionist leaders' activities resulted in the growth and ultimate recognition of the United States as the apparent number one world power.

INTERNAL POLITICAL CONFLICT
AT CENTURY INTERVALS

Three men were presidents in times of great inter-party political conflict and confusion regarding the direction in which the United States should proceed. The first of these faced not only the rise of political disagreement, but the initial espousal of "states' rights", still a factor in internal American political conflict. George Washington, the first of the presidents, Grover Cleveland (2nd term), and William Jefferson Clinton faced similar cycles of bitter internal conflict at century intervals.

THE 1790S

During George Washington's first term as president (1789 - 1793) conflict arose between conservatives and liberals, regarding the organization and operation of American government under the newly adopted Constitution. The leader of those considered conservatives was Washington's Secretary of Treasury, Alexander Hamilton of New York; the leader of those viewed as liberals was Washington's Secretary of State,

Thomas Jefferson of Virginia. This conflict between cabinet members was especially significant, since the United States government had only four department secretaries at the time; the other two were the Attorney General and the Secretary of War.

By the end of Washington's first term, internal conflict had increased to the extent that both Hamilton and Jefferson resigned. The conflict intensified during Washington's second term as president (1793 - 1797), with the conservatives becoming known as the Federalists, and the liberals as the Democratic Republicans. The major element in the conflict of views was the question of the powers and scope of the federal government versus the degree of independence and powers of the individual states. The heart of the conflict was between the states with economies based more on agricultural wealth and slavery, and those states having greater interest in commercial and industrial activities.

Although a plantation owner and a slave owner, George Washington leaned toward Alexander Hamilton's view of government, more than that of Thomas Jefferson, an ardent supporter of the French Revolution of 1789. A national bank proposed by Hamilton was established during Washington's administration.

Washington carefully maintained United States neutrality in the growing European conflict between England and France following the French Revolution. Although France had supported the American colonies during the American War for Independence, neutrality was a wise course of action for the fledgling United States in the 1790s, in view of the power of Great Britain.

THE 1890S

A century later in 1893, the Democrat President Grover Cleveland faced significant conflicts surrounding the nature and scope of American capitalism. Having defeated the bid of Republican Benjamin Harrison for re-election in 1892, Cleveland began his second term as the 24th president (1893 - 1897). The election of 1892 is interesting because of the participation of the Populist Party's presidential nominee, James Weaver of Iowa, who supported free coinage of silver and other economic reforms. The vice-president in Cleveland's second term was Adlai Stevenson of Illinois (a native of Kentucky).

As president, Cleveland again opposed high Republican-supported tariffs, but with less success than in his first term as 22nd president. The Depression of 1893 came during Cleveland's term. Cleveland supported a gold standard and opposed the free coinage of silver sought by the Populists, who represented American farmers. During this time Cleveland called out federal troops to end the bitter Pullman car labor strike that began in Chicago against the railroad companies. Cleveland's action alienated many Democrats. The result was that Cleveland left office in 1797, discredited by his own Democratic Party.

THE 1990S

In 1992, a century after Cleveland's election to a second term, William Jefferson Clinton of Arkansas, the Democratic Party candidate for the presidency, defeated the bid of Republican George H. W. Bush for re-election. In this election, too, a strong third party candidate emerged: Ross Perot of Texas. Perot's original home was Texarkana, Texas, only a few miles from Clinton's early boyhood home in Hope, Arkansas.

Clinton, the 42nd president, like George Washington two centuries earlier, served two terms (1993 - 1997 and 1997 - 2001). In 1996 Clinton was re-nominated by the Democrats and defeated Robert Dole of Kansas, the Republican Party nominee for the presidency. Albert Gore of Tennessee served as vice-president in both of Clinton's terms.

An economic slowdown in 1992 paralleled the economic depression of 1893 during Grover Cleveland's second term as president. The result was that Clinton's terms were marked by increased conflict with the increasingly conservative Republicans in Congress, led by Newton Gingrich of Georgia. The philosophical political conflict between the Democrats and Republicans had been increasing since Republican Barry Goldwater's campaign for the presidency in 1964, but had become more intense during Republican Ronald Reagan's terms as president in the 1980s.

Although Clinton failed to secure adoption of a national health plan, his two terms were generally successful. Significant is the fact that when Clinton left office, the budget deficit was quite small. Unfortunately, during Clinton's presidency Communist Serbia's wars with former subjugated groups in the Balkan Peninsula presented problems for both Europe and the United States.

CYCLICAL PARALLELS

Interesting parallels exist among the presidents in the eras of internal political conflict, having occurred at century intervals. Political conflict was prominent in both of the two term presidencies of George Washington (especially his second term) and William Clinton's presidency, and the second one-term presidency of Grover Cleveland. During Washington's first term, philosophical disagreements between Thomas Jefferson and Alexander Hamilton led to the formation and leadership of the Democratic Republicans and the Federalists respectively. During Washington's two terms (1789 - 1797) the most powerful politician in New York was George Clinton, who served many years as Governor of New York and became a Democratic Republican.

Both William Jefferson Clinton and Grover Cleveland faced strong conservative opposition in Congress. Both were accused of inappropriate activities earlier in their careers. Cleveland admitted fathering an illegitimate child earlier in his life. Clinton faced impeachment proceedings as a result of his affair with a White House staff member. The Clevelands retired to Princeton, New Jersey, south of New York City. The Clintons now live just north of New York City, and Hillary Rodham Clinton has served as New York's US Senator, as well as Secretary of State during the Obama administration.

William Jefferson Clinton, the Democrat president (1993 - 1997 and 1997 - 2001) offers three cyclical parallels. Clinton's first election as president in 1992 came two centuries after George Clinton was third in electoral votes in the 1792 presidential election. William Jefferson Clinton was a Rhodes Scholar; Thomas Jefferson, leader of the Democratic Republicans in the 1790s was recognized as a man of wide ranging interests and great intelligence.

Clinton's original name was Blythe, but he was adopted by his stepfather whose surname was Clinton. William Jefferson Clinton is a persuasive speaker much like William Jennings Bryan, the Democrat presidential nominee one century earlier in 1896 and 1900, who gained fame as an orator.

BITTER PRESIDENTIAL CONTESTS
AND THEIR CONSEQUENCES

Three men served as president during times of increasingly bitter political conflict surrounding their presidential elections. Doubts regarding the direction of America's policies toward other nations also characterized their presidencies. The three were John Adams, William McKinley, and George W. Bush.

1796 AND 1800

In 1796 John Adams of Massachusetts, a Federalist, who had served two terms as Washington's vice-president (1789 - 1793 and 1793 - 1797), won the electoral vote over Thomas Jefferson of Virginia, leader of the Democratic Republicans. Because Adams was a member of a Federalist faction, Alexander Hamilton (the leader of the Federalists) secretly supported Thomas Pinckney of South Carolina (the intended Federalist vice-president) to be elected as president. However, Pinckney was only third in the electoral vote, thwarting the hopes of Hamilton and his followers that Pinckney would gain the presidency.

John Adams, the 2nd president, faced constant difficulties during his term in office (1797 - 1801), due to the European conflict between Great Britain and France. War with France was narrowly averted, but Anglophiles in the United States (some of them in his own faction) were critical of Adams. Unfortunately, Congress adopted the Alien and Sedition Act, making criticism of the president and the government illegal. This further reduced Adams' chance for re-election as president in 1800.

Adams termed his nomination of John Marshall of Virginia (a Federalist) as Chief Justice of the US Supreme Court his greatest contribution to American democracy. As Chief Justice for 35 years, Marshall moved the previously less significant Supreme Court to its position as the third major branch of US government. (John Roberts, appointed Chief Justice by President George W. Bush, is also young enough to serve as Chief Justice for 35 years.)

Having gained the second largest number of electoral votes in the election of 1796, the Democratic Republican Thomas Jefferson of Virginia became vice-president. As vice-president (1797 - 1801) and leader of the Democratic Republicans, Jefferson opposed most of Federalist John Adams' efforts as president

In 1800, Alexander Hamilton of New York, leader of the Federalists openly supported Charles Cotesworth Pinckney of South Carolina for the presidency, instead of John Adams. Consequently Adams' bid for re-election in 1800 ended with his defeat in the electoral vote by both Thomas Jefferson of Virginia, leader of the Democratic Republicans, and Aaron Burr, a Democratic Republican of New York.

Jefferson had intended that Burr would be his vice-president. Because Jefferson and Burr received an equal number of electoral votes, Burr refused to step aside for Jefferson. The result was a protracted conflict in the US House of Representatives that was settled only when Hamilton exerted influence to make Jefferson the third president. Hamilton did this because he trusted Burr less than Jefferson, Hamilton's avowed enemy.

The post-election conflict between Thomas Jefferson and Aaron Burr in 1800 was paralleled by that between George W. Bush and Albert Gore in 2000. Albert Gore, the Democratic Party nominee and loser in the disputed 2000 presidential election, became a major American leader of efforts to combat global warming, unlike the unsavory later history of Aaron Burr, the losing candidate two centuries ago.

1896 AND 1900

In 1896, a century after John Adams' election, the Democratic Party, now including the Populists, nominated William Jennings Bryan of Nebraska for president. Bryan was nominated following his famous "Cross of Gold" speech at the Democratic Party convention. The farmers wanted more money in circulation, and he supported free coinage of silver. The Republicans nominated William McKinley of Ohio, whose name was on the McKinley Tariff Act, passed during Benjamin Harrison's term as president. McKinley defeated Bryan in the election of 1896 and became the 25th president. The vice president in McKinley's first term (1897 - 1901) was Garret Hobart of New Jersey, long active in both politics and business. Hobart died in office in 1899.

McKinley's first term witnessed the sinking (cause still unknown) of the US battleship Maine in the harbor of Havana, Cuba. In the Spanish-American War that followed, the United States quickly defeated the declining Spanish Empire, both in the Atlantic Ocean and Pacific Ocean sectors. As a result, Cuba gained the independence it had sought from Spain, while Puerto Rico became an American territorial possession. The Philippine Islands became an American colony, after the United States government put down a 5-year long insurrection seeking Philippine independence. In 1945, at the end of World War II, the United States finally granted independence to the Philippines.

In 1900, the Republican Party re-nominated William McKinley, who again defeated the Democratic Party nominee William Jennings Bryan. As a result of his land-slide victory, McKinley said that he was now president of all the American people.

Only a few months after beginning his second term as president in 1901, McKinley was assassinated by an anarchist. Theodore Roosevelt of New York, vice president in McKinley's second term, succeeded to the presidency. Roosevelt's nomination for vice president had been strongly supported by New York Republicans at the 1900 Republican Party convention. Although a Republican, Roosevelt had proved to be too liberal for the Republican political powers in New York, who wanted him out of the state.

2000 AND 2004

In 2000, the Republican Party presidential nominee George W. Bush of Texas, son of George H. W. Bush, defeated Albert Gore of Tennessee, the Democratic Party nominee. Gore was vice-president during William Clinton's two terms as president (1993 - 2001). The US Supreme Court settled the conflict over the election result in the State of Florida.

Richard Cheney of Wyoming, who had broad experience in both politics and business, was elected in 2000 as George W. Bush's vice-president. Cheney became the most powerful vice-president in American history. Cheney and Donald Rumsfeld, soon appointed Secretary of Defense, had been long-time leaders in the Republican Party and became a strong force in the Bush presidency.

During the first term of George W. Bush, the 43rd president (2001 - 2005 and 2005 - 2009), Islamic terrorists flew two airliners into the World Trade Center in New York City, and another into the Pentagon in Washington, D.C. An attempt by the Al-Qaeda terrorists to divert a fourth airline flight was foiled by the passengers, who died with the terrorists when the airplane crashed in western Pennsylvania.

One major effort of the Bush administration was to suppress the Al-Qaeda terrorist efforts by removing the Taliban regime from power in Afghanistan. The Taliban had gained power after Communist Russia was forced to end its long occupation of Afghanistan. The Bush administration's efforts resulted in an awkward stalemate and protracted military efforts in Afghanistan to suppress Al-Qaeda terrorist activities.

Following an erroneous conclusion that Iraq possessed "weapons of mass destruction", the Bush administration organized an invasion of Iraq, where the regime of Saddam Hussein was eliminated. Terrorist activities, the conflict between the Sunni and Shiite portions of the Iraqi population, and the desire of the Kurdish people in the northern part of the country for autonomy, continue to present problems in Iraq, despite the election of a US backed government.

In the United States, a Homeland Security Department was established to prevent terrorist activities. The Patriot Act and Military Commissions Act, providing broader investigative powers and harsher control of captured terrorists, was reminiscent of the Alien and Sedition Act, passed during the presidency of John Adams in 1797 - 1801.

In 2004, the Republican Party again nominated George W. Bush for president and Richard Cheney for vice-president. Bush defeated the Democratic Party presidential nominee John Kerry of Massachusetts (like John Adams, a man from Massachusetts) in another close election. A Democratic Party challenge of the voting results in the State of Ohio was considered but not pursued.

The challenges of George W. Bush's first term continued into his second term. He was unable to enforce peace in either Afghanistan or Iraq. Military action by Georgia in 2008 against separatist area South Ossetia led to a forceful response by Russia in both South Ossetia and Abkhasia, another separatist area of Georgia. Russia also warned against NATO missile locations in Central Europe, reviving Cold War sentiments between the United States and Russia. Rapprochement between the European Union and Ukraine and Georgia exacerbated these tensions. The autumn of 2008 brought a major economic crisis both in the United States and around the world.

CYCLICAL PARALLELS

Over 200 years ago President John Adams (1797 - 1801) used the danger of war with Great Britain as a rationale for limiting constitutional rights via The Alien and Sedition Act. Vice President Thomas Jefferson opposed Adams because he favored the French Revolution and wanted to replace Adams as president in 1801. Approximately 100 years later, President William McKinley (1897 - 1901 and 1901 -) used unsubstantiated rumors regarding "The Sinking of the Maine" as a catalyst for embarking upon the Spanish-American War. In George W. Bush's presidencies (2001 - 2004 and 2005 - 2009) his administration used the terrorist attacks of September 11, 2001, to justify the Patriot Act and the invasion of Afghanistan. Never substantiated suspicions of "weapons of mass destruction" were used to justify a "regime change" in Iraq.

The cycle of bitter presidential contests at about century intervals resulted in the election of presidents who allowed the catalyst of public fear to promote or support their political actions. Their failures to be open and honest concerning their actions resulted in a shadow being cast upon their presidencies.

A 4-YEAR TIME OFFSET

After 200 years the century-long cycles in the elections and presidencies have encountered a variation, a 4-year offset in time. This may be due to the 4-year cyclical provision concerning presidential elections included in the United States Constitution. The result is that George W. Bush's conservative presidency offers a cyclical parallel to the presidencies of John Adams and William McKinley, but does not offer a cyclical parallel to those of Thomas Jefferson (1801 - 1805 and 1805 - 1809) and Theodore Roosevelt (1901 - 1905 and 1905 - 1909).

Therefore, this review will continue with the presidencies of Thomas Jefferson through that of Jimmy Carter (1977 - 1981). This will allow later discussion of the 2008 presidential election, with the 4-year off-set in mind.

GIFTED LEADERS AT CENTURY INTERVALS

Two men, a century apart in time, were presidents when the United States began to be a greater influence in the world. Both were unusually gifted leaders, and in their times as president both took advantage of the possibilities in both internal affairs and in foreign relations. The two are Thomas Jefferson and Theodore Roosevelt.

1801

Thomas Jefferson of Virginia became the third president and served two terms (1801 - 1805 and 1805 -1809). The vice-president during Jefferson's first term was Aaron Burr of New York, as Jefferson had planned. However, as a result of the Jefferson - Burr conflict in the 1800 election, Burr was not nominated for vice president in Jefferson's second term. Also Burr had killed Alexander Hamilton in a duel early in 1804, and was in flight from justice in New York and New Jersey, prior to the Democratic Republican presidential nomination in 1804.

As a result of the Jefferson/Burr electoral vote conflict in 1800, the 12th Amendment became a part of the US Constitution. That amendment revised the Electoral College voting procedures, to avoid such an electoral vote conflict occurring again.

During the 1804 election, Jefferson easily gained a second term as president, defeating the Federalist nominee Charles Cotesworth Pinckney of South Carolina. The Democratic Republican nominee for vice-president in 1804 was George Clinton of New York (1805 - 1809).

During Jefferson's first term as president, the purchase of the Louisiana Territory from Napoleon of France doubled the land area of the United States. Jefferson dispatched the Lewis and Clark expedition not only to seek a convenient route to the Pacific Ocean, but also to establish a claim to land area on the Pacific Coast, in competition with Great Britain and Spain. Jefferson also sent a force to defeat the Barbary pirates in North Africa, who had demanded tribute from American ships

Jefferson's second term was less successful. Prosecution of Aaron Burr for conspiring to form a separate southwestern republic was unsuccessful. Like John Adams, Jefferson faced the problem of conflict between Great Britain and France. His attempted use of a trade embargo, to bring the two enemies to terms, failed; it was unpopular in the United States, especially in New England where trade was impacted.

1901

A century later in 1901, Theodore Roosevelt became the 26th president and completed the 1901 - 1905 term that President McKinley had begun. Theodore Roosevelt, at age 42, was the youngest man ever to become president. In 1904 Roosevelt was nominated by the Republican Party; he defeated the conservative Democratic Party nominee Alton Parker of New York. Parker was defeated by a larger margin than William Jennings Bryan had been defeated by William McKinley in the two previous elections.

Charles Fairbanks of Indiana, a native of Ohio, was Roosevelt's vice-president (1905 - 1909). Fairbanks supported William Howard Taft against Theodore Roosevelt in the campaign of 1912.

As president, Theodore Roosevelt confronted and defeated a continuing insurrection in the Philippine Islands following the Spanish-American War. Although a conservative supporter of business, Roosevelt continued to be a proponent of government reform, and an opponent of business practices he considered improper. He supported enforcement of the Sherman Anti-Trust Act, passed in 1890, and sided with the United Mine Workers, who sought an 8-hour workday and higher wages. Roosevelt was the first American president to take strong action in conservation matters, establishing a system of national parks.

In 1903 Roosevelt secretly supported the revolt of Panama from Colombia, because Colombia had rejected a treaty giving the United States the right to build a canal across Panama. Roosevelt believed that the Panama Canal was a necessary route for sea traffic. He also negotiated an end to the Russo-Japanese War in 1905, and helped to reconcile differences between France and Germany over control of Morocco in North Africa.

CYCLICAL PARALLELS

Thomas Jefferson and Theodore Roosevelt were two able leaders a century apart. Jefferson was not only highly intelligent, but also far sighted. His great accomplishments were in expanding American territory and making possible greater American power. They ensured his position as one of America's greatest presidents.

Generally, Theodore Roosevelt was a moderate conservative, attempting to combine what he considered to be the best of conservative and progressive views. His desire for fairness, combined with vigorous action, made for success as president, both within the United States and in foreign affairs. Roosevelt was intelligent, a historian, and a prolific writer. It is not surprising that artist Gutzon Borglum carved the faces of Thomas Jefferson and Theodore Roosevelt on Mt. Rushmore, in the Black Hills of South Dakota, along with those of George Washington and Abraham Lincoln.

LEGAL MINDS AND MAJOR WARS AT CENTURY INTERVALS

These time periods reflect two major concerns within and between nations: the rule of law and dispensation of justice within and between nations. Wars are the failure to resolve international conflicts and maintain peace. The end of open warfare requires efforts to gain a just peace.

Three American presidents have served at century intervals, when extraordinary legal decisions have been needed. They were James Madison, William Howard Taft, and Woodrow Wilson. Barack Obama, the current president, faces similar problems.

JAMES MADISON

In 1808 James Madison of Virginia, the Democratic Republican candidate, defeated the Federalist Charles Cotesworth Pinckney of South Carolina, who lost a second presidential election. Madison, the 4th president, had been a member of the Continental Congress and he, Alexander Hamilton, and John Jay had been key figures in the formulation of the United States Constitution. Madison led the defense when the Constitution was attacked in Virginia by anti-Federalist forces led by Patrick Henry. Madison had been Jefferson's Secretary of State, and his presidential candidacy was endorsed by Jefferson.

The vice-presidential nominee in 1808 was George Clinton of New York, who had been Jefferson's second vice-president (1805 - 1809). Clinton died in office in 1812 before his second four-year term as vice-president was completed.

Madison's presidency (1809 - 1813 and 1813 - 1817) was plagued by foreign policy concerns. The Non-Intercourse Act to end trade with both Great Britain and France was a failure, like the trade embargo during Jefferson's administration. France gained Madison's promise to lift the embargo against any power that observed America's neutrality. Meanwhile, war-hawks in Congress pressed for war with Great Britain, hoping to acquire control of Canada. Madison was unable to prevent the war with Britain, which began in 1812.

Although the war was not popular, Madison was re-nominated by the Democratic Republican party in 1812. In the election he defeated DeWitt Clinton of New York, a nephew of George Clinton, who was nominated by a separate Democratic Republican Party caucus, but was supported by the Federalists. The vice-president in Madison's second term was Elbridge Gerry of Massachusetts, who served (1813 - 1814) until dying in office. (Earlier when Elbridge Gerry was governor of Massachusetts he supported a congressional re-districting act that so obviously favored Democratic Republicans that the term "gerrymandering" came into existence.)

During the War of 1812, efforts by the United States to take Canada failed. Washington, D. C. was occupied by the British and the White House burned, but Baltimore was successfully defended. Fortunately for Madison, naval successes in the Great Lakes area offset army defeats, and the Treaty of Ghent officially concluded the war in a standoff. A bright spot for the US Army was General Andrew Jackson's defeat of the British at New Orleans, before either of the opposing armies had learned that the war was over.

The already weakened Federalist Party, which had not supported the war, was effectively destroyed by the war and was no longer a significant political force.

James Madison did not oppose the demise of the first national bank, established during George Washington's presidency, but he approved the establishment of a second national bank in 1816. James Madison was the last surviving member of the Constitutional Convention, which was convened in the late 1780s. He died at age 86 in 1836.

WILLIAM HOWARD TAFT

In 1908, having served nearly 8 years as president, Theodore Roosevelt declined to pursue re-nomination; the Republican Party nominated William Howard Taft of Ohio, Roosevelt's political heir, for the presidency. Taft had served as a US circuit court judge and as High Commissioner for the Philippine Islands, before serving as Roosevelt's Secretary of War. The Republican vice-presidential nominee was James Sherman of New York, who died in office in 1912. The Democrats turned again to William Jennings Bryan of Nebraska as their presidential nominee, but he failed for a third time to be elected.

Although he initiated more anti-trust suits as president than Roosevelt, Taft as 27th president (1909 - 1913) pursued more conservative policies. His support of a more protectionist tariff alienated mid-western Republicans. He supported expansion of American business interests overseas, but was less supportive of conservation; this led to a break with conservationists and Roosevelt.

Consequently, in 1912 former president Theodore Roosevelt announced that he would oppose Taft for the Republican Party nomination. When narrowly defeated by Taft at the Republican Party convention, Roosevelt and his followers formed a Progressive Party which came to be known as the "Bull Moose" Party.

(THOMAS) WOODROW WILSON

(Thomas) Woodrow Wilson of New Jersey (a native of the South) gained the Democratic Party presidential nomination in 1912. Before entering politics, Wilson had risen to president of Princeton University. Upon entering politics, Wilson, as governor of New Jersey, pushed a program of political and economic reforms. The Democrat vice-presidential nominee in 1912 was Thomas Marshall of Indiana, who served in both of Wilson's terms (1913 - 1917 and 1917 - 1921). In the election of 1912, Wilson, the 28th president, handily defeated Theodore Roosevelt of the "Bull Moose" Party. Taft, the Republican Party nominee, ran a distant third.

In his first two years as president, Wilson pushed several major governmental reforms through Congress, including reduction of tariffs to the lowest level since before the Civil War. In 1916 he sent an expedition, under General John Pershing, into Mexico to capture the bandit Pancho Villa. That expedition was withdrawn in 1917, and the Mexican government of Carranza was recognized.

World War I, which had begun in Europe in 1914, drew Wilson's attention in 1915 when German submarine warfare began. The sinking without warning of two British ships, also carrying American passengers, led Wilson to send strong warnings to Germany. Germany pledged not to sink ships without warning and attempting to save lives. Germany abided by its pledge during the last part of 1916.

In 1916 Wilson and Marshall were re-nominated by the Democratic Party on the basis of having kept the United States out of the European war. Wilson defeated the Republican Party nominee Charles Evans Hughes, who was an Associate Justice of the Supreme Court from 1910 to 1916. Wilson became the first Democrat since Andrew Jackson to win a second consecutive term as president.

Following a revolution that deposed the Tsar of Russia early in 1917, Russia withdrew as an ally of Great Britain, France, and Italy in the war against Germany, Austria/Hungary, and the Ottoman Empire. The Communists, under the leadership of Nicholas Lenin took power in Russia in the autumn of 1917.

In January 1917 Germany announced renewed submarine warfare, and in April 1917 the United States entered the war on the side of the allies Great Britain, France, and Italy. In entering the war, Wilson felt that both sides in Europe had been responsible for the war, and in January 1918 he announced his plans for a League of Nations to resolve international disputes. Following the end of the war in November 1918, the allies agreed at the peace treaty to establishment of the League of Nations, but forced Germany into an agreement to "war guilt" and heavy reparations. The empires of Austria/Hungary and the Ottoman regime were dismembered and divided into smaller nation-states.

Wilson campaigned for US Senate approval of the peace treaty, but objections mainly from Republicans, were raised. Wilson might have gained approval, but he opposed all the changes proposed. On a speaking tour to support his position, Wilson suffered a stroke which left him disabled. An amended version of the treaty was rejected, after Wilson urged Democrat loyalists to oppose the treaty. Although the United States Senate never approved the treaty, Wilson's concept of a new world order remained as guidance for American foreign policy.

CYCLICAL PARALLELS

The rule of law and dispensation of justice were advanced by Madison, Taft, and Wilson. As presidents all three exerted long term influence in the organization and operation of American government. Approximately a century apart, both Presidents Madison and Wilson were forced into decisions concerning war as part of a major European conflict.

William Howard Taft is the only president who has also served as Chief Justice of the United States Supreme Court (1921 - 1930). Charles Evans Hughes, the Republican nominee defeated by Wilson in 1916, was Supreme Court Chief Justice (1930 - 1931), succeeding Taft. Alton Parker, the losing Democratic Party presidential candidate in 1904, had served as Chief Judge of the New York Court of Appeals.

GOOD TIMES AT CENTURY INTERVALS

The time periods reviewed here were not as good as slogan titles might indicate. However, they were peaceful and prosperous from the viewpoint of most Americans living in those times. Peaceful times in politics were based on great weakness on one political side and unusual strength on the other. The presidents a century apart were James Monroe, John Quincy Adams, Warren Harding, and Calvin Coolidge.

"THE ERA OF GOOD FEELING"

In 1816, following the era of the Napoleonic wars, the Democratic Republicans nominated James Monroe of Virginia for president. Monroe easily won the electoral vote over the last Federalist Party candidate, Rufus King, active in politics first in Massachusetts and later in New York, and became the 5th president. In 1820 Monroe was re-nominated at the Democratic Republican caucus. With neither intra-party nor inter-party opposition, Monroe won an overwhelming electoral victory. Daniel Thompkins of New York was vice-president in both of Monroe's terms (1817 - 1821 and 1821 - 1825).

Monroe's terms have been called the "Era of Good Feeling". An 1818 agreement ended conflict in the Great Lakes area with Great Britain. East and West Florida were acquired from Spain (1819 - 1821). The Missouri Compromise (1820) settled the first serious conflict over slavery peacefully. The compromise allowed Missouri to enter the Union as a slave state and Maine to enter as a free state, but banned slavery above 36 Degrees and 30 Minutes North in the Louisiana Purchase Territory.

In Monroe's second term, the Monroe Doctrine asserted that there would be no further European colonization or European intervention in the affairs of American governments. In turn America would abstain from political affairs in Europe.

The lack of inter-party opposition in the election of 1820 resulted in increased intra-party rivalries in 1824. At least five prominent Democratic Republicans sought the party nomination for president. William Crawford of Georgia, a supporter of "states' rights" who had sought the Democratic Republican Party nomination in 1816, won endorsement in a congressional caucus, but the others refused to accept that caucus decision as binding.

"GOOD FEELING" EBBS

In the 1824 election, Andrew Jackson of Tennessee won the popular vote. He also won the electoral vote, but did not gain the majority required by the Constitution. The election then went to the House of Representatives, which had to choose among the top three in electoral votes - Andrew Jackson, John Quincy Adams, and William Crawford. The Twelfth Amendment of the Constitution, the contingency procedure, eliminated Henry Clay of Kentucky who had run fourth. However, Clay used his influence as Speaker of the House of Representatives and gave support to Adams for president.

John Quincy Adams of Massachusetts, son of John Adams the 2nd president, became the 6th president (1825 - 1829). Adams chose John Calhoun of South Carolina, the fifth of the Democratic Republican candidates, as his vice-president. Andrew Jackson immediately began his campaign to win the next presidential election in 1828. Jackson's actions made evident that the Democratic Republican "Era of Good Feeling" was coming to an end.

John Quincy Adams was well prepared to become president. He had wide experience in foreign affairs, including being Monroe's Secretary of State, and had served in the US Senate. His presidency was less than successful because of his somewhat aloof personality. Adams supported a broad program of improvements, including the Chesapeake and Ohio Canal, but they were largely un-funded due to opposition in Congress. He supported a protective tariff in 1828, which increased tension between the Northern and Southern states.

"THE RETURN TO NORMALCY"

A century later, in 1920 the Republicans sought a "Return to Normalcy" following WWI and nominated Warren Harding of Ohio for president and Calvin Coolidge of Massachusetts for vice-president. In the election they easily defeated the Democrat nominees, James Cox of Ohio for president and Franklin Roosevelt of New York for vice-president. Harding was the 29th president (1921 - 1923). Harding, a newsman before entering politics, was not well prepared for the presidency.

The Republicans neither rejected the new government agencies brought in by Woodrow Wilson nor his internationalism. They emphasized the need for government and business partnership, and economic interaction with Europe. Harding supported high tariffs and high taxes for internal development. The Washington Naval Conference of 1921 - 1922 set limits on the construction of battleships by the major powers.

However, there were rumors of scandals in the administration before Harding's death of a heart attack in 1923. The most notorious scandal revealed later was that of Secretary of the Interior Albert Fall's secret leasing of the Teapot Dome naval oil reserves in return for millions of dollars in bribes.

Upon the death of Harding, Calvin Coolidge became the 30th president (1923 – 1925 and 1925 - 1929). Although termed "Silent Cal", Coolidge was quite successful in dealing with the media. He sought to reduce taxes and federal spending, and to block liberal legislation. His popularity with the public led to his nomination by the Republicans in 1924 and an easy victory over the Democrat nominee John Davis of West Virginia. Coolidge's vice-president (1925 - 1929) was Charles Dawes of Illinois (a native of Ohio).

"NORMALCY" DECLINES

In Coolidge's second administration, government - business partnership was enhanced, even among government regulatory agencies. Agriculture received less attention, and farmers continued to face the decline in agricultural prices that set in after World War I. The Geneva Conference to limit construction of naval cruisers was unsuccessful, but through the international banking community the restructuring of

Germany's finances, with a new schedule for war reparation payments, was arranged.

CYCLICAL PARALLELS

Peaceful times were characteristic in both the "Era of Good Feeling" years of Presidents James Monroe and John Quincy Adams (1817 - 1829) and the "Return to Normalcy" years of Presidents Warren Harding and Calvin Coolidge in 1921 - 1929. There was obvious near non-existence of an opposition conservative party in the electoral period of 1816 - 1828 and evident weakness of the opposition Democratic Party during the 1920 - 1928 electoral years. Both Adams and Coolidge were from New England and embodied change to conservative governmental actions.

MEN FROM THE WEST AT CENTURY INTERVALS

Two presidencies portray the geographic growth of the United States from thirteen former British Colonies situated along the Atlantic Ocean to a great nation extending to the shore of the Pacific Ocean. Even their rise to success, both as private citizens and as politicians attest to the population growth and rapid rise in influence of the United States. The presidencies are Andrew Jackson's first term (1829 - 1833) and Herbert Hoover's single term (1927 - 1933). Andrew Jackson was the first president from area west of the Appalachian Mountains and Herbert Hoover was the first president from area west of the Rocky Mountains.

ANDREW JACKSON

In 1828 Andrew Jackson of Tennessee (a native of North Carolina), an able organizer and politician, defeated the bid of John Quincy Adams for re-election. John Calhoun of South Carolina, vice president under John Quincy Adam (1825 - 1829), was elected vice president again. Adams' vice presidential candidate was Richard Rush of Pennsylvania.

Jackson, elected the 7th president (1829 - 1833 and 1833 - 1837), had been successful in business, active in politics, and had led forces against the Native Americans in the South. He served as a general in the War of 1812 - 1815 and his defeat of the British at New Orleans in 1815 made him a national hero. Later he led forces against the Seminole Indians in Florida in 1818.

As president Jackson believed that many federal government jobs had become life-time positions. He replaced some of the occupants with political supporters, a move that initiated the "spoils system" in following presidencies.

Jackson and Vice President Calhoun disagreed in 1832 over South Carolina's "nullification" of the Tariff Act of 1832 initiated by Henry Clay. Calhoun argued that a state should have the right to reject or nullify a law passed by Congress. Jackson and others believed this would destroy the Union. Jackson threatened to arrest Calhoun and Calhoun resigned the vice presidency in 1832. In 1833 Henry Clay arranged a congressional compromise on the tariff which had been passed, and South Carolina repealed its "nullification" act.

Jackson's actions at the time of the conflict with John Calhoun led to the beginning of the modern Democratic Party, distinct from the Democratic Republicans. Jackson is recognized as the founder of the Democratic Party.

HERBERT HOOVER

A century after Jackson's election in 1828, Calvin Coolidge chose not to run for re-election. The Republican Party nominated Herbert Hoover of California (reared in Iowa and Oregon) for the presidency. For the vice presidency they chose Charles Curtis of Kansas. The Democrats nominated Alfred Smith of New York for the presidency.

Hoover easily won the election and became the 31st president (1929 - 1933). Hoover, a mining engineer, had become a successful and wealthy international businessman. In World War I he first directed food relief for Belgium, and then led food administration for the United States in Europe. After the Armistice of 1918, he continued as director of American relief efforts in Europe before entering politics. During the Harding and Coolidge administrations, Hoover served effectively as Secretary of Commerce.

In 1929, the first year of Hoover's term, the stock market crashed and the Great Depression struck the United States. Economists believed that, as in past depressions, all that was necessary was to reduce spending. Hoover believed the depression was so great that it was necessary for government to work with commercial interests. However the actions Hoover took in loans and public works were insufficient. Efforts to stop the naval arms race, and to get Japan to leave the puppet state it established in Manchuria, failed. The term of Hoover can be considered the real end of the Republican Party's "Return to Normalcy" era.

CYCLICAL PARALLELS

The two Men from the West, Jackson and Hoover, came to the presidency by different routes. Jackson's father died before Jackson was born. Jackson joined the American Revolutionary Army at age 13. He rose to general in the War of 1812 -1815 after being involved in conflicts with Native Americans in the South, land speculation, law and politics in Tennessee.

Hoover was orphaned as a boy in Iowa and reared by an uncle and aunt in Oregon. He attended Stanford University, became a mining engineer, and gained wealth through mining activities. He gained fame as a result of his relief activities during World War I, before entering politics.

Jackson of Tennessee was the first president from the Old West, the land west of the Appalachian Mountains. Hoover of California was the first president from the Far West, the land west of the Rocky Mountains. Both were able men. Jackson, the liberal, was successful as president. Hoover, the conservative, was president when the Great Depression began, and with ways necessary to lessen its impact not yet accepted, his presidency was doomed to failure.

ABLE LIBERALS A CENTURY APART

Andrew Jackson (2nd term) followed by Martin Van Buren and a century later by Franklin Roosevelt (first two terms) are honored as liberals who devoted their political lives to support of equality for American citizens. Van Buren is less well known as a president but his political efforts later in life in the anti-slavery movement clearly portrayed his liberal beliefs.

ANDREW JACKSON AND MARTIN VAN BUREN

In 1832, Andrew Jackson, re-nominated by the Democrats, was re-elected by defeating Henry Clay of Kentucky (a native of Virginia), the nominee of the National Republicans (a conservative faction of the former Democratic Republican Party). Martin Van Buren of New York was nominated and elected to serve as vice president (1833 - 1837) under Jackson. Henry Clay had picked John Sergeant of Pennsylvania to run with him.

During the 1832 presidential campaign, Jackson vetoed a bill to renew the charter of the second bank of the United States created by Congress in 1816. Jackson thought banks encouraged speculation, and he favored hard money over paper money. Defeat of the bank proposal helped Jackson win re-election.

Henry Clay and his followers supported renewal of the bank charter. Clay had raised the issue even though the bank charter was not due to expire until 1836. Clay thought his proposal would help to defeat Jackson, but Jackson easily won re-election.

As in his first term (1829 - 1833), Andrew Jackson was a strong and successful president in his second term (1833 - 1837). He was the first president to go over the heads of Congress to seek public support for his positions.

In 1836 Jackson decided against a third term and supported the Democratic Party nomination and the election of his vice president Martin Van Buren. Colonel Richard Johnson of Kentucky, an Indian fighter, was nominated for vice president.

The former National Republican faction, now loosely re-organized as the conservative Whig Party, was again led by Henry Clay of Kentucky. Believing that he could not beat the Democrats himself Clay, with the help of John Calhoun of South Carolina, supported a favorite-son strategy. The Whigs selected three candidates - Hugh White of Tennessee, a moderate "states-rights" man; General William Henry Harrison of Ohio (a native of Virginia); and Daniel Webster of Maine, once a Federalist and now a Clay ally.

The Democrat nominee Martin Van Buren won the election with Harrison leading among the Whig candidates. Van Buren was the 8th president (1837 - 1841). Unfortunately, soon after he entered office there was a severe economic downturn, the Money Panic of 1837. The fiscal policies pursued earlier by Andrew Jackson may have contributed to this, and Van Buren believing in limited government, was unable to do much to slow the downturn. His failure to support the proposed annexation of Texas, which had gained independence from Mexico in 1836, was unpopular, particularly in the South.

FRANKLIN ROOSEVELT

In 1932, a century after Jackson's re-election, Franklin Roosevelt of New York, the Democratic Party nominee easily defeated the bid of the Republican Herbert Hoover for re-election as president. Franklin Roosevelt, the 32nd president (1933 - 1937, 1937 - 1941, 1941 - 1945 and 1945 -), was a distant cousin of Theodore Roosevelt, the 26th president. The vice president in Franklin Roosevelt's first two terms (1933 - 1941) was John Garner of Texas.

Roosevelt had campaigned on a "New Deal" to combat the Great Depression. Roosevelt initiated several liberal actions. He pushed banking reform, aid for the farmers and public works projects. In a more conservative action, he supported stimulation of economic activity through a system of industrial and business self-government and regulation.

Prior to his campaign for a second term, and as a result of criticism from the left, Roosevelt initiated broader public works programs and the Social Security Act. In the 1936 presidential election Roosevelt won a land-slide victory over the Republican Party candidate, Alfred Landon of Kansas.

As a result of Supreme Court decisions limiting some of his programs Roosevelt, in his second term, attempted to increase the size of the Supreme Court to 18 members. This attempt at "court packing" was defeated in Congress.

CYCLICAL PARALLELS

A century apart, both Andrew Jackson and Franklin Roosevelt were able and powerful presidents. Both Jackson and Roosevelt were clever politicians and were accused of dictatorial actions. Like Roosevelt, Martin Van Buren was recognized as an astute politician. All three presidents were liberals in their approach to political issues. Both Van Buren and Roosevelt were of Dutch ancestry in the Hudson River Valley in New York.

The elections of 1832, 1836, 1932 and 1936 reflected the serious weakness of the opposing conservative parties. The Money Panic of 1837 came in Van Buren's term. The Great Depression in the 1930s continued through Roosevelt's first two terms. A small upturn in the economy in 1937 was temporary and the depression continued until the onset of spending for World War II.

WAR AND THE RISE OF AMERICAN POWER AT CENTURY INTERVALS

The "40s" in two centuries have been times of war resulting in increasing American power and influence. In contrast, beginning in the "40s" and intensifying in the "50s" there has been increased internal political conflict enhanced by disagreement regarding the place of African-Americans in American society. Presidents during these time periods were William Henry Harrison, John Tyler, James Polk, Franklin Roosevelt (3rd and 4th terms) and Harry Truman. Internal conflict involved Vice Presidents John Tyler and Henry Wallace.

THE MEXICAN WAR 1846 - 1848

In 1840 William Henry Harrison of Ohio (a native of Virginia), who had served as a general in the Indian wars in the Old Northwest Territory and in the War of 1812, was nominated for the presidency by the Whigs. Harrison's nomination was due to his having been the top vote getter among the three Whig candidates that Henry Clay and John Calhoun had supported in the effort to defeat President Martin Van Buren in 1836.

Henry Clay, the chief arranger of the 3 - Whig candidacies, had become known as the "Great Compromiser" following the Missouri Compromise of 1820. Clay had moved step by step from being a follower of Thomas Jefferson to being the leader of the conservatives in the 1830s and 1840s. Henry Clay is without doubt one of the more clever and astute politicians who sought but never gained the presidency of the United States.

William Henry Harrison defeated the bid for re-election of Martin Van Buren whose chances for a win had been destroyed by the Money Panic of 1837. Nominated for Vice President was John Tyler of Virginia. Harrison, the 9th president (1841 -), died of pneumonia one month after his inauguration as president.

John Tyler, the 10th president (1841 - 1845), was the first "Accidental President". The Constitution was vague concerning succession, but Tyler set a useful precedent by quickly assuming responsibility as president after Harrison's death.

Earlier Tyler, originally a Democratic Republican, had moved toward the Whigs because he opposed many of Andrew Jackson's policies. The Whigs had hoped to capture Southern votes with Tyler's vice-presidential nomination. Tyler soon evidenced his strong support for "states' rights" and rejected most of the Whig Party agenda, causing the Whigs to eject him from their party.

Tyler twice vetoed Whig bills to establish a national bank, and all but one of his cabinet members resigned. He approved an act speeding settlement on the western frontier, and saw final settlement of the Maine - Canada boundary and the boundary with Canada as far west as the Rocky Mountains. Tyler led the push to annex the Republic of Texas, a preliminary to the Mexican War, but now a man without a party he chose not to run for re-election in 1844.

Former president Martin Van Buren of New York was again a leading candidate for the Democratic Party nomination in 1844, but he was opposed by Southern Democrats who favored annexation of Texas. James Polk of Tennessee (a native of North Carolina) was a surprise Democratic Party nominee and won the 1844 presidential election by defeating the Whig Party nominee, Henry Clay of Kentucky (a native of Virginia). In the very close election of 1844, Henry Clay's chances to win were lessened by his waffling on the annexation of Texas, and by the candidacy of James Birney of the anti-slavery Liberty Party that opposed slavery and gained some of the Whig votes.

James Polk was the 11th president (1845 - 1849). His vice-president was George Dallas of Pennsylvania. Polk sought to buy California from Mexico, but was unsuccessful due to Mexico's refusal to accept the recent American annexation of Texas, a Mexican territory before it gained independence in 1836. In 1846 Polk ordered troops to occupy a disputed

Texas border area, and the Mexican War began. In 1848 Mexico, after being defeated in the war, was forced to cede to the United States the California Territory (which comprised all or parts of the future states of California, Arizona, New Mexico, Nevada, Utah, Colorado, and Wyoming).

Polk had campaigned in 1844 on the goal of a "54 - 40" boundary between the United States and British Western Canada. The 49th Parallel was agreed on as the boundary.

Polk had promised, when accepting the Democratic Party nomination in 1844, that he would not run for re-election. He kept his promise, becoming the first elected president not to seek a second term.

WORLD WAR II 1941 - 1945

In 1940, a century after William Henry Harrison's election as president, the Democratic Party nominated Franklin Roosevelt for an unprecedented third term. As in 1916 the election was shadowed by war in Europe. Roosevelt had done nothing to groom a successor and accepted a "draft" to be the candidate. John Garner of Texas did not seek a third term as vice-president, and many in the Democratic Party were unhappy with Roosevelt's choice of Henry Wallace of Iowa as the vice-presidential candidate.

The Republican Party had two leading candidates for the presidential nomination: Robert Taft of Ohio (son of former President William Howard Taft) and Thomas Dewey of New York. However, a newcomer to politics, Wendell Wilkie of Indiana, a business man who had been a Democrat and supporter of the "New Deal" until 1939, gained a surprise Republican Party nomination.

In 1940 Wilkie agreed with Roosevelt on the need to aid the Allies in Europe, but dismissed Roosevelt's pledge to stay out of the war and predicted that the United States would be at war by April 1941. Roosevelt defended his actions and won the election decisively, although not like the landslide victory of 1936.

Early in 1941 the Lend Lease Act allowed the allies in Europe to obtain military supplies from the United States without cash payments. The United States placed some US Navy vessels in the Atlantic Ocean war zone by the spring of 1941.

In the Pacific Ocean area, fearful that the United States would not allow it to expand southward to gain oil and other resources, Japan attacked the US Navy at Pearl Harbor in December 1941. The history of World War II from that date forward is familiar to most adult Americans.

In 1944 Roosevelt received a fourth Democratic Party nomination for the presidency without significant opposition. Facing strong opposition to re-nomination of Henry Wallace for vice president, Roosevelt accepted the Democratic Party convention nomination of Harry Truman of Missouri for the vice-presidency. In the 1944 election Roosevelt defeated the Republican Party candidate Thomas Dewey of New York. Before the Republican Party convention, the 1940 Republican nominee Wendell Wilkie had withdrawn as a candidate after a loss in the Wisconsin primary. Dewey supported the war effort, but sought a change of administration after Roosevelt's 12 years in office.

Franklin Roosevelt died in office in April 1945, having been elected 4 times and after serving more than 12 years as president. In 1947 Congress approved a Constitutional Amendment, which was ratified in 1951, that declared that no president could be elected more than twice nor could a president serve more than half of his predecessor's term and be elected more than once. This was in line with the precedent established by George Washington in 1796, when he refused a third term as president. Andrew Jackson followed that precedent in 1836, when he refused to run again.

Upon Franklin Roosevelt's death in 1945, Harry Truman became the 33rd president (1945 - 1949 and 1949 - 1953) of the United States. Roosevelt had not taken Truman into his confidence, but Truman proceeded with the presidency and World War II ended with the formal surrenders of Germany in May and Japan in September 1945.

Truman sought to carry out Roosevelt's post-war plans, but with advice from the State Department assumed a stronger position toward Communist Russia. Between 1946 and 1949 disagreements with expansionist Communist Russia escalated and the Cold War began.

The Truman Doctrine provided needed economic and military assistance to Greece and Turkey. In 1947 the Marshall Plan for reconstruction of Europe was announced. George Marshall, had been US Army Chief of Staff during WW II, and Truman had appointed him Secretary of State.

In 1948, after Russia imposed a blockade of ground access from the west from the Russian zone of occupation in Germany, Truman ordered an air lift of supplies to Berlin. In 1949 the West German Republic was recognized and the United States became a member of NATO (the North Atlantic Treaty Organization).

KOREAN WAR 1951 - 1953

In 1948 Truman was nominated for the presidency by the Democratic Party and defeated Thomas Dewey of New York, the Republican candidate in one of the great upset victories of history. Also defeated were the Southern Democrats, who formed a "Dixiecrat" Party led by Strom Thurmond of South Carolina, and a "Progressive Party", led by Henry Wallace of Iowa.

Truman's greatest crisis came with the June 1950 attack by Communist North Korea, a protégé of Communist Russia, which occupied almost all of South Korea. The Inchon landing led by General Douglas MacArthur, who had been the administrator of the occupation of Japan since 1945, reversed the course of the war. However, the general led forces (now designated as United Nations) all the way to the Yalu River boundary between North Korea and Communist China. That brought China into the war and the Chinese and North Koreans pushed the combat line back into South Korea. General McArthur criticized the administration for not widening the war with China, and Truman relieved him from duty in April 1951.

The combat line in Korea was pushed back to a location near the original division line between North and South Korea and bitter conflict continued in that area. Armistice negotiations which began in July 1951, remained unresolved the remainder of Truman's administration and until July 1953. Armistice was delayed due to North Korean and Chinese demands that each of their POWs be returned to the particular units in which they had served so that they could be questioned.

Truman advocated a "Fair Deal" and universal health insurance, but most of his programs were defeated by a conservative Congress. The Department of Defense, National Security Council and Central Intelligence Agency were created during Truman's administration. Racial segregation in the US Armed Forces was ended by Truman in 1947.

Republican Senator Joseph McCarthy of Wisconsin and other right-wingers were making charges regarding internal subversion. There were calls for impeachment because of Truman's firing of General MacArthur.

Americans grew tired of the Korean War and Truman became unpopular. Although he was not barred by the 22nd Amendment to the Constitution from seeking re-election in 1952, Truman decided against it.

CYCLICAL PARALLELS

The death of William Henry Harrison in 1841 paralleled the death in 1945 of Franklin Roosevelt, who won the 1940 election, and the death in 1944 of Wendell Wilkie, the losing candidate in 1940. Vice-Presidents John Tyler and Henry Wallace were not popular with the parties that elected them vice president in 1840 and 1940 respectively.

James Polk, who was elected president in 1844, and Harry Truman, who became president in 1945, proved to be strong and decisive presidents. Both greatly enhanced American power and prestige during war and in foreign relations actions. Both presidents decided against seeking re-election. These two presidents are said to share a common although distant family ancestry.

GENERALS AT CENTURY INTERVALS

At century intervals men, who had been successful American Army generals, were honored by being called to serve as presidents. They were Presidents Zachary Taylor and Dwight Eisenhower. Taylor died in office, and Eisenhower suffered two serious illnesses while in office. Their vice presidents are interesting. Millard Fillmore, who succeeded Taylor as president, was less than laudable as a politician after leaving the presidency. Richard Milhouse Nixon, who was Eisenhower's vice president, became president later in his life but was the first president to resign in disgrace.

THE 1850S

When James Polk did not seek re-election in 1848 the Democratic Party nominated Lewis Cass of Michigan, who had served in the Indian wars and the War of 1812, and favored "squatter sovereignty" for territories. Martin Van Buren, formerly a Democrat, entered the presidential race as the candidate of the Free Soil Party which wished to ban slavery in newly acquired areas. The Whigs turned to their successful 1840 strategy and nominated another popular general, Zachary Taylor of Kentucky (a native of Virginia). Taylor, a career soldier since 1808, had led an American army in northern Mexico and won a great victory over Mexican General Santa Anna at Buena Vista in 1847, near the end of the Mexican War. Taylor won the presidential election and became the 12th president (1849 - 1850). His vice-president was Millard Fillmore of New York.

Although a slave owner, President Taylor opposed the extension of slavery and the Compromise of 1850, which brought California into the Union as a state and applied "popular sovereignty" to the other western areas taken from Mexico. He said that states could not secede and threatened force if necessary to preserve the Union. The slavery debate was going on when President Taylor died suddenly in 1850.

Upon Taylor's death Millard Fillmore became the 13th president (1850 - 1853). Fillmore reversed Taylor's policy and supported the Compromise of 1850. One provision of that Compromise required the federal government to return run-away slaves. Fillmore's agreement with this position caused Northern Whigs to prevent his nomination for the presidency in 1852. The split in the Whig Party over the Compromise of 1850 led to the party's demise after 1852.

In 1852 the Whig Party chose another war hero, General Winfield Scott who had led the campaign which took Mexico City during the Mexican War. Scott had been defeated by General Zachary Taylor for the Whig nomination in 1848. Scott resisted the growing anti-immigrant and anti-Catholic prejudice in the most conservative portion of the Whig Party which culminated later in the American or "Know Nothing" Party. However, Scott's alliance with anti-slavers cost him in the election.

The Democrats settled on a "dark horse" Franklin Pierce of New Hampshire who had served in the Mexican War and risen to the rank of brigadier general. Pierce thought the Compromise of 1850 would settle the slavery problem. Pierce's popular majority vote gave him a substantial electoral vote victory, making him the 14th president (1853 - 1857). William King of Alabama was Pierce's vice-president (1853 - 1857). The anti-slavery Free-Soil Party ran John Hale of New Hampshire, but he received half as many votes as Martin Van Buren had as the Free-Soilers candidate in 1848.

Franklin Pierce was a New England politician who soldiered only in the Mexican War. His term as president seems to have been the beginning phase of the long internal struggle of the American Civil War and might well be included in the later discussion of "Years of War and Bitter Internal Conflict".

In 1853 Franklin Pierce at age 43 was the youngest man elected to become president. In 1854 he supported the Kansas-Nebraska Act proposed by Democrat Senator Stephen Douglas of Illinois that resulted in two separate territories, and provided that the issue of slavery would be decided in each of them by popular vote or "popular sovereignty". Fighting that broke out in Kansas in the 1850s was the preliminary to the Civil War. Pierce was unsuccessful as president, and was the first elected president who was not considered for re-election by his party.

THE 1950S

A century after Pierce's 1852 election by defeating General Winfield Scott, the Republican Party nominated another career soldier, General Dwight Eisenhower of Kansas, for the presidency. Eisenhower had commanded the Allied Forces in Europe in World War II. The Democratic Party nominee in 1952 and 1956 was Adlai Stevenson of Illinois. The Republican vice-presidential nominee in both 1952 and 1956 was Richard Milhouse Nixon of California. Eisenhower won both elections easily and was the 34th president (1953 - 1957 and 1957 - 1961).

As president Eisenhower believed in limited federal government. He turned over to the states off-shore oil rights, opposed most public works projects, tried to overturn agricultural price supports, and opposed provision of medical insurance. But he provided for expansion of Social Security and sought an increase in the minimum wage. The Health, Education and Welfare Department (HEW) was created and legislation obtained for construction of the St. Lawrence Seaway and the Interstate highway system.

Eisenhower disliked arch-conservative Republican Senator Joseph McCarthy, who was still making charges of internal subversion, but Eisenhower shared the belief that national security was endangered. He signed an order allowing the firing of security risks. Senator McCarthy finally brought about his own downfall.

Eisenhower supported voting rights, but he did not send US Army troops to support racial integration at the Little Rock, Arkansas Central

High School until rioting broke out and the Arkansas governor withdrew the National Guard.

Eisenhower followed existing foreign policy, but felt there had been too much reliance on ground forces and based containment of Communism on the threat of using nuclear arms. In Korea, after long negotiation, an armistice with Communist China and Communist North Korea finally was gained in 1953. Eisenhower was unable to assist a 1956 anti-Communist revolution in Hungary, and decided against helping the French, who were forced to sue for peace after their defeat by the Vietnamese Communists at Dien Bien Phu in North Vietnam.

Eisenhower did recognize the rise of Third World nationalism; when Great Britain and France invaded Egypt to prevent it from nationalizing the Suez Canal, Eisenhower forced the two nations to withdraw their troops. Eisenhower was the first president barred by the 22nd Amendment to the Constitution (1951) from seeking a third term.

CYCLICAL PARALLELS

Just over a century apart, successful generals were elected as presidents: Zachary Taylor in 1848 and Dwight Eisenhower in 1952. The increasingly divisive conflict over slavery in the 1840s and 1850s, prior to the Civil War, was paralleled by the rising complaints about racial segregation in the South in the 1940s and 1950s.

Zachary Taylor died in office in 1850 and was succeeded by Millard Fillmore. Dwight Eisenhower suffered two serious illnesses in the 1950s. If he had died Richard Milhouse Nixon would have become president. Fillmore was not nominated by the Whig Party in 1852, and one can wonder what actions Richard Milhouse Nixon might have taken if he had become president in the 1950s.

General Winfield Scott, the Whig candidate who lost to Franklin Pierce in 1852, was one of the two great Mexican War heroes. Mexico was defeated when General Scott's army defeated the Mexican Army defenders and occupied Mexico City. A century later General Douglas McArthur led the American army troops in the Pacific sector in World War II, became the administrator of the occupation of Japan, experienced a great battle win at Inchon, and then suffered a defeat in North Korea.

YEARS OF BITTER INTERNAL CONFLICT AND WAR AT CENTURY INTERVALS

The American Civil War between the North, seeking to preserve the Union and the secessionist South, was preceded and followed by years of bitter internal political conflict. A century later internal conflict arose again over the place of African-Americans in American society. War came again but this time the war was between two segments of a nation in Southeast Asia with the United States supporting the losing side, South Vietnam.

American presidents in the two eras a century apart are Franklin Pierce (discussed above), James Buchanan, Abraham Lincoln, Andrew Johnson, John Kennedy and Lyndon Johnson. Interesting vice presidents were Andrew Johnson, Lyndon Johnson, Hannibal Hamlin and Hubert Humphrey.

THE 1850S AND 1860S

In 1856 the Democratic Party ignored Franklin Pierce, and turned to James Buchanan of Pennsylvania as their presidential nominee. John Breckenridge of Kentucky was the vice-presidential nominee. James Buchanan had entered politics as a Federalist and opposed the War of 1812 - 1815 before joining the army in 1814. Later he became a Democratic Republican, and then a Democrat supporter of Andrew Jackson. He had sought the nomination in 1852, when Franklin Pierce gained it. The Democratic Party endorsed "popular sovereignty" and warned of Southern secession if the Republican Party, formed in 1854, won the election.

The Whig Party had splintered after its loss in 1852. The American Party, the most conservative wing of the old Whig Party, divided into two groups after its 1855 convention. The most conservative group of the American Party was anti-immigrant and anti-Catholic. It became known later as the "Know Nothing" Party. One group of the American Party voted to support the Kansas-Nebraska Act which repealed the Missouri Compromise and supported "popular sovereignty". A small group did not and left the American Party to join the recently formed Republican Party.

The Republican Party had been formed in 1854 by the Free Soilers, the anti-slavery Democrats, and a part of the former Whig Party. The small group from the American Party which joined the Republican Party after 1855 was termed the "Conscience Whigs".

Millard Fillmore, no longer supported by the Northern Whigs, refused to join the Republican Party formed in 1854. In 1856 Fillmore ran unsuccessfully for president representing the anti-immigrant and anti-Catholic American Party known as the "Know Nothing" Party.

In 1856 the Republican Party nominated John Fremont for the presidency. Fremont was a soldier whose unusual career led to his being well known. Fremont first gained fame following his report on his explorations of the Far West, guided by the renowned scout Christopher "Kit" Carson. Fremont's maneuvers during the seizure of California during the Mexican War made him more famous. Being a son -in-law of US Senator Thomas Hart Benton of Missouri may have been helpful too.

Despite the pro-slavery attack on the anti-slavery town of Lawrence, Kansas, the assault with a cane by a Southern Congressman on a Northern Senator in the US Senate chamber earlier in 1856, and the unpopularity of the Kansas - Nebraska Act, voters evidently put the preservation of the Union first. The Democrats won the election of 1856 by sweeping the South and narrowly winning several Northern states. Thus James Buchanan became the 15th president (1857 - 1861).

SLAVERY BECOMES THE ISSUE

Buchanan had won the election of 1856 but slavery now became the major issue. The Republicans demanded immediate admission of Kansas as a free state, repeal of the Fugitive Slave Act, and abolition of slavery in the District of Columbia.

As president, Buchanan tried to appease both the North and South. He opposed slavery but did not think it could be abolished under the Constitution. He supported the Supreme Court's 1857 Dred Scott decision, which ruled that no slave could be a citizen and that Congress could not outlaw slavery in any territory. He supported admitting Kansas as a slave state, opposed by many Northern Democrats. By 1860 neither Northern nor Southern wings of the Democratic Party wanted to re-nominate Buchanan.

In 1860 the Democratic Party split into two groups. For president the Northerners nominated Stephen Douglas of Illinois and the Southerners nominated John Breckenridge of Kentucky, Buchanan's vice president. The Constitutional Union Party nominated John Bell of Tennessee for president. Abraham Lincoln, reared in Kentucky and Indiana before moving to Illinois with his family at age 21, was nominated for president by the Republican Party in 1860. Lincoln, formerly a Whig, had become a Republican in 1854. Hannibal Hamlin of Maine was the Republican vice-presidential nominee in 1860.

In the 1860 election Lincoln won 40 percent of the popular vote and the Electoral College majority, and became the 16th president (1861 - 1865 and 1865 -). Stephen Douglas was second in popular vote but fourth in the Electoral College vote. Bell prevailed in the states of Virginia, Kentucky and Tennessee. Breckenridge swept the rest of the South.

Eleven Southern states seceded from the Union, and the American Civil War began in April 1861. Lincoln increased the size of the military and ordered a blockade of Southern ports. Lincoln feared abolishing slavery would cost support of the states that had not seceded; therefore, when Lincoln issued the Emancipation Proclamation in 1862, it provided that slaves living in states in rebellion in January 1863 would be free. The Civil War continued but after initial losses in the East the Union armies finally began to win the war in the East as well as they had in the West.

In 1864 Lincoln was re-nominated by the Republican Party. Andrew Johnson of Tennessee, a pro-Union Democrat, was nominated for vice-president. The Democrats nominated for President General George McClellan, whom Lincoln had twice removed from army command. Lincoln won the election in 1864 with 65 percent of the popular vote and entered his second term (1865 -).

The last Southern armies, led by Generals Robert Lee and Joseph Johnston, surrendered in April 1865. Only a few days later, after President Lincoln said in a speech at the White House that Blacks should have the right to vote, he was assassinated by John Wilkes Booth, a Southern sympathizer. Andrew Johnson of Tennessee, a native of North Carolina, then became the 17th president (1865 - 1869).

Abraham Lincoln had intended to be somewhat lenient and bring the eleven Southern states back into the Union. However, many conservative Republicans did not favor this approach.

Andrew Johnson had believed that the Constitution protected slavery, but he had opposed secession when Tennessee left the Union in 1861. He had been the only Southern senator to remain in the US Senate when his state seceded. Later Lincoln appointed Johnson military governor of Tennessee. Lincoln also asked for Johnson's nomination for vice-president in 1864.

As president Johnson attempted to follow Lincoln's plan to bring the eleven Southern states which had seceded back into the Union. "Radical Republicans" wanted more stern treatment of the South. Johnson vetoed many of the congressional bills; Congress overrode some of his vetoes.

Johnson challenged the Tenure of Office Act passed by Congress, when he fired Secretary of War Edwin Stanton. Congress then initiated impeachment proceedings. The House of Representative voted for impeachment, but in the Senate trial Johnson was acquitted by a one vote margin

COLD WAR DANGER, STRUGGLE FOR CIVIL RIGHTS, THE VIETNAM WAR

THE 1960S

In 1960, a century after Abraham Lincoln won the presidential election, John Kennedy of Massachusetts defeated Hubert Humphrey of Minnesota (a native of South Dakota) for the Democratic Party nomination. Kennedy won a narrow victory in the 1960 presidential election, defeating Richard Nixon, the Republican Party nominee, who was completing eight years as Dwight Eisenhower's vice-president (1953 - 1961). Kennedy became the 35th president (1961 - 1963). At 43 he was the youngest president ever elected. His vice-president was Lyndon Johnson of Texas.

Kennedy was charismatic and popular with the American public. He led in the founding of the Peace Corps to provide technical guidance and aid to people in poor countries. He began more support for the Civil Rights Movement, which had begun to gain strength in the 1950s.

The Cold War between the United States and Communist Russia and Communist China had become more perilous. In 1961 Kennedy supported an effort to overthrow Communist Fidel Castro, who had come to power in Cuba in 1959 after a revolution. Plans for the effort had been prepared in the Eisenhower administration, but the invasion of Cuba by Cuban exiles was a disaster.

In 1961 Communist Russia announced it was turning over Allied access routes into West Berlin to Communist East Germany. A similar threat in 1958 had been ended by Eisenhower through diplomacy. Kennedy mobilized military reserves and asked for greater military appropriations. Communist East Germany built the Berlin Wall to end the movement of refugees from Communist East Germany to the West.

In 1962 it was discovered that Communist Russia was placing missiles in Cuba. The United States instituted a blockade and prepared for an air strike and invasion of Cuba. Communist Russia agreed to remove the missiles if the United States would not invade Cuba. The Cuban missile crisis was the most dangerous time of the Cold War; it could have led to nuclear war. Kennedy sent 16,000 troops to South Vietnam, the first step in United States involvement in the war there.

In November 1963 Kennedy was assassinated in Dallas, Texas, and Lyndon Johnson became the 36th president (1963 - 1965 and 1965 - 1969). Johnson, a very ambitious and astute politician, worked to become a great president. His "Great Society" programs were perhaps the greatest reforms by any president. Determined to not be a president who lost a war, he sent a large number of troops to aid South Vietnam.

In 1964 the Democratic Party nominated Lyndon Johnson for president, and he won a land-slide victory over the Republican nominee Barry Goldwater of Arizona. Hubert Humphrey of Minnesota (a native of South Dakota) became the Democrat Vice President (1965 - 1969). In Johnson's full term as president (1965 - 1969) the Voters Rights Act of 1965 became the most significant part of his "Great Society", with the 24th Amendment to the Constitution (1964) prohibiting poll taxes and other measures used in the South to control elections.

During the 1964 election Johnson depicted the arch-conservative Republican Barry Goldwater of Arizona as a war hawk, but in 1964 he got Congress to authorize a presidential war to stop the Communists in Vietnam. Johnson and his advisers believed that the Russian-supported Communist aggression must be stopped in Vietnam, or it would spread to other countries in Southeast Asia.

During the Vietnam War Johnson continued to expand the number of troops in South Vietnam, and began air war against Communist North Vietnam. Despite the "Great Society" programs, the Democratic Party followers of Robert Kennedy opposed Johnson's administration. The Tet offensive by North Vietnam early in 1968, although defeated, brought out stronger opposition to the war. With no end of the war in sight, by 1968 Johnson's presidency was destroyed.

In 1968 after Johnson was almost upset in the New Hampshire Democratic primary by Eugene McCarthy of Minnesota, an opponent of the war, Robert Kennedy entered the race for the Democrat nomination for president. Johnson then announced that he would not seek re-nomination or re-election.

Soon thereafter Martin Luther King Jr., the great civil rights leader of the 1960s, was assassinated in Memphis, Tennessee. Not long after that presidential candidate Robert Kennedy, after defeating Eugene McCarthy in the California primary election, was assassinated in Los Angeles, California.

Lyndon Johnson gained an open housing law and a truth in lending law, but members of his party were rebelling against him. Therefore, Johnson chose not to attend the Democratic Party convention in Chicago, which was accompanied by rioting by those opposing the Vietnam War. Hubert Humphrey, Johnson's vice president, received the Democratic Party nomination in 1968.

TIMING OF WARS A CENTURY APART

Open North-South conflict began in Kansas in 1856 and the American Civil War was fought from 1861 to 1865. The eleven Southern states which had seceded were occupied during the "Reconstruction" era following the war until 1879. Following the Civil War the US Army pursued conquest of the Native Americans in the Great Plains and Great Basin in the West.

US Army troops were sent to South Vietnam in 1962; the war in Vietnam started more slowly than the American Civil War but continued for a longer period of time. Near the end of the war, US Army troops were sent westward into Cambodia. The Vietnam War brought opposition to the military draft and great internal conflict to America. During the American Civil War there was rioting in New York City regarding the military draft for the Union Army.

CYCLICAL PARALLELS

Franklin Pierce and John Kennedy were the youngest presidents when elected. James Buchanan and John Kennedy were of Irish descent. Abraham Lincoln and John Kennedy were great orators and debaters; both were assassinated. Both Abraham Lincoln and Lyndon Johnson were war-time leaders (one successful and one not), and both greatly advanced the interests of African-Americans. Both were unusually ambitious, able, and liberal politicians.

Abraham Lincoln's first Vice President was Hannibal Hamlin. Lyndon Johnson's Vice President was Hubert Humphrey.

During Abraham Lincoln's presidency Frederick Douglass, was a leader of the black Americans and a great writer and speaker. During Lyndon Johnson's presidency Martin Luther King, Jr., leader of the African-Americans and a great orator, was assassinated.

Both Andrew Johnson and Lyndon Johnson were Southerners. Neither man agreed with the beliefs dominant in the Southern states during the key years of their lives. Andrew Johnson was almost impeached by the Republicans who had elected him. Lyndon Johnson was effectively driven from office by his Democratic Party.

UNFORTUNATE LEADERS AT
CENTURY INTERVALS

Two men of great ability, Ulysses Grant and Richard Nixon, who lived a century apart, are interesting because of unusual successes and failures encountered during their lives. The four vice presidents who served with them, Schuyler Colfax, Henry Wilson, Spiro Agnew, and Gerald Ford, are also interesting. Colfax and Agnew because of their unusual oratorical gifts, and Wilson and Ford because of name changes earlier in their lives.

ULYSSES GRANT

In 1868 the Republican Party (soon to be self-designated the Grand Old Party or GOP) unanimously nominated for president General (Hiram) Ulysses Simpson Grant of Illinois (a native of Ohio), the most successful commander of the Union Army during the Civil War. The

Democratic Party, not having much of their Southern base, rejected Andrew Johnson and nominated Horatio Seymour of New York for the presidency. Grant won the presidential election and became the 18th president (1869 - 1873 and 1873 - 1877). He gained most of the votes cast by the Freedmen in the Southern states then under "Reconstruction". The vice president in Grant's first term (1869 - 1873) was Schuyler Colfax of Indiana (a native of New York).

As president, Grant at first refused to make appointments until the Tenure of Office Act was repealed. Congress under Senate leadership removed only some of the worst parts of the Act. Then Grant followed the advice of the Senate in making executive branch appointments. Thus Grant and his cabinet came to be dominated by a group of powerful conservative Republican Party senators.

Grant did propose some reforms to improve government administration and refused to spend funds for purely private interests, but being somewhat inexperienced in politics and believing in limited government, his two terms as president were marked by a time of profiteering and corruption. As he had learned and improved as an army leader, Grant improved as a president, but his improvement came too late.

As early as 1870 more liberal Republicans became dissatisfied with Grant, and began urging an end to radical "Reconstruction" and removal of troops from the South. In May 1872 a group of more liberal Republicans convened in Indiana and nominated Horace Greeley, a New York newspaperman, for president. Greeley, a native of New Hampshire, was an odd combination of conservative and liberal.

A month later the conservative Republicans met in Philadelphia and nominated Grant for a second term. The party chose Henry Wilson of Massachusetts (a native of New Hampshire) for vice president. When the Democratic Party convened in Baltimore it voted to accept the platform and the candidates of the liberal Republicans (Horace Greeley and Benjamin Gartz-Brown).

In 1872 Grant was re-elected by defeating Horace Greeley. Shortly before the election Greeley's wife died and Greeley believing himself badly defeated, although not worse than several losing candidates before him, was depressed. Soon he was placed in a sanatorium and died in three weeks. At the February 1873 electoral vote counting, Democrat electors gave some Greeley votes to the Democrat vice presidential nominee and some to several other Democrats.

In 1870 in Grant's first term as president, the states ratified the 15th Amendment to the Constitution, forbidding denial of suffrage due to race. However, Democrats began to regain control of Southern states. Grant did not feel strong enough politically to stop this, and the last of the "Carpetbagger" or Black governments in the Southern states disappeared shortly after Grant left office in 1877 at the end of his second term. During Grant's second term the Money Panic of 1873 further damaged his presidency.

RICHARD NIXON

In 1968, a century after Grant's election as president, the Republican Party nominated Richard Nixon for president. Nixon had been Dwight Eisenhower's vice president for 8 years, but had been defeated in 1960 by Democrat John Kennedy in the closest popular vote for president since the Cleveland - Harrison vote in 1888. Nixon had also been defeated by the incumbent governor of California in a 1962 election. Nixon won the 1968 election and became the 37th president (1969 - 1973 and 1973 - 1974). Nixon narrowly defeated the Democratic Party nominee Hubert Humphrey of Minnesota (a native of South Dakota). The Republican vice president nominee in 1968 was Spiro Agnew of Maryland.

As president Nixon began a phased withdrawal from South Vietnam while increasing military aid to the South Vietnamese army and intensifying bombing of North Vietnam. He called for reduced American presence in Asia, and quieted the anti-war movement in America until he sent American forces in Vietnam westward into Cambodia, which re-ignited the anti-war movement for a time.

In 1971 Nixon surprised the world by sending Henry Kissinger, his national security advisor, to Communist China to arrange for a presidential visit in 1972. The goal was improvement of relations with Communist China, then involved in disputes with Communist Russia. Nixon also went to Moscow where he and Leonid Brezhnev, the Communist Russian leader, signed the first Strategic Arms Limitation Treaty (SALT 1).

Control of inflation and reduction in unemployment seemed to be succeeding by 1972. In 1972 Nixon was re-nominated for president, and overwhelmed George McGovern of South Dakota, the Democratic

Party candidate, in the election. Spiro Agnew of Maryland was again Nixon's running mate, and was vice president (1968 - 1972 and 1973 -). In October 1973 Agnew was forced to resign as vice president or face prison for taking bribes.

WATERGATE

Just before the 1972 presidential election five persons connected with the Committee to Re-elect Nixon were arrested for burglary in the Democrat National Committee headquarters in the Watergate Building in Washington, DC. The burglary gradually became a major issue for the Nixon Administration. Attempts to cover up any involvement with the five persons arrested made the matter worse. In the end, demands for his impeachment led to Nixon's resignation as president on August 8, 1974. This presidential history is still a topic of discussion.

Even before the Watergate affair, which began in 1972, Nixon's presidency was attacked in Congress. In 1973 Congress passed over Nixon's veto, the War Powers Act requiring the president to report within 30 days on any commitment of American troops abroad and to withdraw the troops in 60 days if the commitment was not approved by Congress.

In January 1973 Nixon announced that Communist North Vietnam had agreed to a cease-fire, but negotiations dragged on. In the Yom Kippur War of October 1973, the Arab states attacked Israel but the United States saved Israel with massive military aid. Increases in the price of oil by the Petroleum Exporting Countries (OPEC) caused inflation and slowed the economy.

CYCLICAL PARALLELS

Presidents Grant and Nixon, who lived a century apart, were sons of men who ran small businesses. Grant went east from Ohio to enter the US Military Academy at West Point, NY. Nixon went east from California to Duke University Law School in North Carolina. Grant served brilliantly as a young army officer in the Mexican War. Nixon rose to Lt. Commander in the Navy in World War II.

Grant's life between the Mexican War and the Civil War was not marked by success. Then he found exceptional success as a general in the American Civil War, but his presidency found him unprepared and proved unfortunate. Nixon gained success early in his political career, but met disappointing defeats in his 1960 and 1962 election campaigns. Nixon finally gained the presidency in 1968, and his first term can be considered successful. His second term ended in disaster.

Both Grant and Nixon were able men. Grant, a great general but lacking in political experience, was president in a time in which many powerful political leaders were either greedy or vengeful or both. Nixon inherited a war accompanied by bitter internal conflict. His undoing was the result of meeting the Democratic Party opposition with suspicion and combativeness.

CYCLICAL PARALLELS IN VICE PRESIDENTS

The vice presidents of Grant and Nixon, a century apart, are especially interesting. Grant's first vice president Schuyler Colfax (1869 - 1873) was not re-nominated in 1872 because a congressional investigation implicated him in corrupt dealings. Colfax left office under a cloud and earned his living thereafter by giving lectures. The departure of Nixon's first vice president Spiro Agnew in 1973 has been discussed above. Agnew was recognized as a very entertaining speaker.

Henry Wilson, Grant's second vice president (1873 - 1875), was defeated in seeking the vice presidential nomination in 1868, but succeeded in 1872. Wilson's original name was Jeremiah Jones Colbath. His name was changed to Henry Wilson by a legislative act when he was age 21. Wilson died in office in November 1875.

Nixon's second vice president was Gerald Ford of Michigan (1973 - 1974) who was appointed to fill the vacancy left by the resignation of Spiro Agnew late in 1973. Ford had been Republican Party leader in the US House of Representatives. He served as vice president until Richard Nixon resigned as president in August 1974. Ford's original name was Leslie Lynch King, Jr. He was not told until he was age 15 that Gerald Rudolph Ford, Sr., his mother's second husband, was his stepfather and not his father. Ford's name was not actually changed to Gerald R. Ford, Jr. until he was almost age 22,

UNEXPECTED PRESIDENCIES

When Richard Nixon resigned, Gerald Ford became the 9th unexpected president and served as president (1974 - 1977). The previous unexpected presidencies were:

1. John Tyler when William Henry Harrison died in office.
2. Millard Fillmore when Zachary Taylor died in office.
3. Andrew Johnson when Abraham Lincoln was assassinated.
4. Chester Arthur when James Garfield was assassinated.
5. Theodore Roosevelt when William McKinley was assassinated.
6. Calvin Coolidge when Warren Harding died in office.
7. Harry Truman when Franklin Roosevelt died in office.
8. Lyndon Johnson when John Kennedy was assassinated.

Of the unexpected presidents only Theodore Roosevelt, Calvin Coolidge, Harry Truman, and Lyndon Johnson were elected to another term as president. John Tyler, Millard Fillmore, Andrew Johnson and Chester Arthur were rejected by their parties. Gerald Ford gained his party's nomination in 1976 but his election attempt failed.

UNUSUAL ELECTION BATTLES
AT CENTURY INTERVALS

A century apart presidents have been elected following unusual election struggles. Rutherford Hayes became president following a questionable 1876 election result and was called the "Selected President". Gerald Ford gained the presidency following his appointment as vice president and the resignation of President Nixon in 1974, and was called the "Un-elected president". Both Hayes and Ford encountered unusual Congressional opposition during their presidency.

A new president, Jimmy Carter, gained the presidency in a very close 1976 election over Gerald Ford. The presidencies of Hayes and Carter are interesting because they began one and two centuries after 1776, the year of America's declaration of independence from Great Britain. The War for Independence was not unanimously supported; some people in the colonies favored continued rule by Great Britain and a number migrated north and became the founders of the province of Ontario in Canada.

THE 1876 ELECTION STRUGGLE

In 1876 a third term for Ulysses Grant was not possible; the corruption during his two terms had become embarrassing to Republican Party leaders. James Blaine of Maine, a party favorite, wanted the nomination but his connections with railroad scandals eliminated him. The Republican Party nominated Rutherford Hayes of Ohio for president and William Wheeler of New York for vice president. The Republicans complained about the "spoils system" and favored holding public officials responsible.

The Democratic Party nominated Samuel Tilden of New York for president and Thomas Hendricks of Indiana as vice president. The Democrats called for end of "Reconstruction" in the South, civil service reform, and for honest men in government.

Both Hayes and Tilden favored hard money and Hayes like Tilden supported removing troops from the South. In the election Tilden won the popular vote and led 184 to 165 in electoral votes. Although 20 electoral votes were still in doubt (7 in South Carolina, 8 in Louisiana, 4 in Florida and 1 in Oregon), Tilden needed only 1 vote to win while Hayes needed all 20. Then Zachariah Chandler, the chairman of the Republican Party National Committee, claimed the 1 electoral vote in Oregon still in doubt, and sent telegrams to secure the 19 votes of the three Southern states (two states - South Carolina and Louisiana were still under "Carpetbagger" rule). The day after the election Chandler simply claimed the Republicans had 185 electoral votes. Three days later President Grant sent more troops into the three Southern states to see that the electoral vote was proper.

The confusion and conflict over the disputed electoral votes in Oregon, South Carolina, Louisiana and Florida lasted from November 8, 1876 until March 2, 1877, one of the darkest periods in American political history. During that time two sets of electoral votes were sent to Washington from each of the three Southern states and Oregon.

The Constitution prescribes the process for congressional counting of electoral votes. The Democratic Party majority in the House of Representatives objected to the president of the Senate reporting the decision on the votes. The Republican majority in the Senate opposed shifting the decision to the House. After weeks the Senate and House agreed to establish an Electoral Commission of 5 senators, 5 representatives and 5 Supreme Court justices. One of the justices was considered to be independent, but then he was elected to the US Senate by the Illinois Legislature. The justice who replaced him was a Republican, expected to be non-partisan. He was not and supported the Republicans on every issue. The Electoral Commission then awarded all 20 disputed electoral votes to Hayes, who thus defeated Tilden 185 to 184, and became known as the "Selected President".

Many Democrats were irate but Samuel Tilden accepted the political decision. Southern Democrats already knew that Hayes was friendly toward them. At a series of secret meetings, Southern Democrat leaders had reached a compromise with Northern Republicans; they agreed to accept the Electoral Commission vote in return for a pledge that Hayes would remove troops from South Carolina and Louisiana, the two remaining Republican "Carpetbagger" governments. In his letter accepting the Republican Party nomination, Hayes had recommended ending military "Reconstruction".

RUTHERFORD HAYES, THE "SELECTED PRESIDENT"

Rutherford Hayes, the 19th president (1877 - 1881), was better prepared for the presidency than Ulysses Grant, and believed in a strong executive branch of government. He worked for revival of the Republican Party in the South, and for voting rights for Blacks in the South. Southern Whites united as Democrats to disenfranchise the Blacks, forcing President Hayes to veto bills which included "riders" intended to limit Black voting rights. The Democrats had a majority in Congress, and the Republicans did not well support Hayes' efforts. The result was racial segregation and "Jim Crow" rule in the Southern states until changes in the South began in the 1950s and 1960s. The first real step was President Harry Truman's termination of racial segregation in the US Armed Forces in 1947.

Among President Hayes appointments was Carl Shurz, a noted proponent of civil service reform, as Secretary of the Interior. This angered Republican Senate leaders, but public support forced them to retreat. Hayes investigation of the New York Customs House brought conflict with Senator Roscoe Conkling of New York (mentioned earlier in this essay) and other US Senators. Hayes eventually won and instituted merit and tenure systems in federal government field offices.

GERALD FORD, THE "UN-ELECTED PRESIDENT"

Gerald Ford became the 38th president (1974 - 1977) following the resignation of Richard Nixon from the presidency on August 9, 1974. Ford was the only person to become both vice president and president without having been elected to either office. Ford had been appointed vice president by Nixon in December 1973 (pursuant to the 25th amendment to the Constitution) following the resignation of Vice President Spiro Agnew in October 1973. Ford, who had served 24 years in the House of Representative and had been Speaker of the House for 8 years, had almost unanimous support for his appointment.

In September 1974 President Ford granted Richard Nixon a full and unconditional pardon for any crimes he may have committed as president. At the same time he granted conditional amnesty to Vietnam War draft dodgers who had fled to Canada and other countries. The pardon of Nixon was costly to Ford in the 1976 presidential election.

The Watergate Affair was costly to the Republican Party in the 1974 mid-term elections. The Democratic Party majority in the House of Representatives was sufficient for the highest over-ride of presidential vetoes since Andrew Johnson's presidency (1865 - 1869).

In 1974 and 1975 President Ford faced a problem of inflation followed by recession. Ford strongly supported the Equal Rights Amendment, and gained passage of the Education for Handicapped Children Act of 1975.

Ford supported an amendment to permit each of the 50 states making the choice on abortion, his position when House Majority Leader regarding the Supreme Court case of Roe v. Wade. Later in life he was pro-choice.

When the North Vietnamese conquered South Vietnam in 1975, Ford ordered the rescue from Saigon, by US Armed Forces, of US citizens and a substantial number of South Vietnamese and other nationals. He continued détente with Communist Russia and Communist China, and gained the Helsinki Accords with Communist Russia. He attended the inaugural meeting of industrialized nations, later enlarged to the Group of Eight and now the Group of Twenty.

After Gerald Ford became president, two attempts were made to assassinate him. These occurred in the autumn of 1975, a century after the death in 1875 of Henry Wilson, President Grant's second vice president.

THE CLOSE ELECTION OF 1976

In 1976, a century after the confused election of 1876, President Gerald Ford (1974 - 1977) reluctantly agreed to run for the Republican Party nomination. His opponent was Ronald Reagan, Governor of California. Reagan said Ford should have done more for South Vietnam, should not have signed the Helsinki Accords, and should not have begun negotiating to cede the Panama Canal, later completed by President Jimmy Carter.

Ford gained the Republican Party nomination at the convention but support for Reagan was so strong that Ford was forced to choose Robert Dole of Kansas as his running mate in place of his appointed vice president Nelson Rockefeller of New York.

In 1976, despite opposition from Ted Kennedy of Massachusetts, the Democratic Party nominated Jimmy Carter of Georgia for president on the first ballot. With more states holding primaries Carter had campaigned nearly two years, winning most of the primaries he entered. He campaigned as a born-again Christian and promised to eliminate secrecy in government and diplomacy and to issue no misleading statements. He called for a balanced budget, strength in military parity with Communist Russia, reduced government waste, tax reform, national health insurance, and an end to discrimination on the basis of race and sex.

Jimmy Carter had risen to Governor of Georgia and was the first Democratic Party nominee from the Deep South to oppose racial discrimination. In this way he, like Gerald Ford, may be considered a parallel to Rutherford Hayes who supported voting rights for the Blacks in the South. Carter chose Walter Mondale of Minnesota to run for vice president.

In the election campaign President Ford supported a strong military defense but Carter won the 1976 presidential election with 50.1% of the popular vote. The election was so close that a shift of less than 25,000 votes in Ohio and Wisconsin which adjoined Gerald Ford's home state of Michigan would have given Ford a majority of the electoral votes.

PRESIDENT FROM THE SOUTH

As the 39th president Jimmy Carter (1977 - 1981) created the Department of Education and the Department of Energy. He supported a national energy policy that included conservation and reduction of foreign oil imports. He completed the return of the Panama Canal Zone to Panama, for which he was criticized. He successfully pursued the Camp David Accords agreement between Israel and Egypt, and the second round of the Strategic Arms Limitation Talks (SALT II) with Communist Russia.

In the last part of Carter's term as president, the United States faced severe inflation and a shortage of fuels. Failure to provide answers to these problems reduced Carter's chance for re-election.

Carter reduced or eliminated United States support for some authoritarian regimes, but continued support for the Shah of Iran. Return of the Shah to power in Iran in 1953 had been aided by the United States. After another revolution deposed the Shah again, a fundamentalist religious regime gained power in Iran.

Carter's final year as president was marred by the takeover of the US embassy in Tehran and the holding of hostages in Iran. An attempt to rescue the hostages failed. The Communist Russia invasion of Afghanistan presented another major problem in Carter's presidency.

President Carter defeated the challenge of Ted Kennedy of Massachusetts for the Democratic Party nomination in 1980, but Carter was defeated in the presidential election by Ronald Reagan of California, the Republican Party nominee.

CYCLICAL PARALLELS

Rutherford Hayes gained the presidency in 1876 after Samuel Tilden accepted defeat in the electoral vote. Hayes was sometimes referred to as "His Fraudulency". Gerald Ford who became president in 1974 after Richard Nixon's resignation was an "Un-elected President".

Prior to his inauguration in 1877, Hayes said he would serve only one term. Gerald Ford reluctantly agreed to run for president in 1976 and was defeated in the election.

Rutherford Hayes' attempts to protect voting right for Blacks in the South were stopped by a Democrat majority in Congress. In the mid-term elections in 1974, less than three months after Ford became president, the Democratic Party increased its House of Representatives majority to one vote more than needed to over-ride a presidential veto. This presented a problem throughout Ford's presidency.

The presidency of Jimmy Carter, Gerald Ford's successor began in 1977. Carter's presidency is interesting because it came two centuries after the last 4 years of the American War for Independence which involved increased conflict and suffering in the Southern British Colonies. Carter's presidency may also be indicative of the 4-year offset in the presidential elections.

Carter's presidency was difficult due to a time of economic inflation, fuel shortages, and the problem of hostages held in Iran. Carter lost the presidential election in 1980 to Ronald Reagan.

James Garfield, discussed earlier in this essay, won the presidential election in 1880 and was assassinated in 1881. In contrast to James Garfield in 1881, Ronald Reagan was fortunate and survived a gun-shot wound by an assassin in 1981.

POSSIBLE EFFECT OF THE 4-YEAR OFFSET

THE 2008 PRESIDENTIAL ELECTION

Parallels in the elections and presidencies of the United States, from the time of American independence in 1781 through the presidential elections of George W. Bush in 2000 and 2004 have been discussed earlier in this essay. It has been noted that a 4-year offset in the century long cycles in American presidencies, has appeared. The result of the offset is that the elections of George W. Bush in 2000 and 2004 offer a parallel to the elections of John Adams in 1796 and William McKinley in 1896 and 1900, but not to those of Thomas Jefferson, in 1800 and 1804 and Theodore Roosevelt as vice president in 1900 and as president in 1904. Therefore, in examining the 2008 presidential election concerning possible parallels with those one and two centuries ago it is necessary to keep in mind the 4-year offset in time cited earlier. The offset could introduce a clear-cut permanent change in the cycle.

THE 2008 REPUBLICAN PARTY NOMINEE

In 2008 John McCain of Arizona (ancestry in Mississippi) gained the Republican Party nomination for president after defeating six other candidates in the primary contests. Earlier in life McCain, son and grandson of US Navy admirals and a graduate of the US Naval Academy at Annapolis, MD served as a Navy Lt. Commander and aviator in the Vietnam War. His plane was shot down and he was a POW in North Vietnam for 5 ½ years. After returning home as a war hero he rose to Captain in the US Navy, before moving west, entering politics, and rising to US Senator from Arizona.

McCain first sought the Republican Party nomination in 2000 but was defeated in a nasty primary contest in South Carolina by George W. Bush, who gained the nomination, won the 2000 election, and became president in 2001. McCain continued service in the Senate after his defeat by Bush, and was moderate enough to be called a "maverick" by more conservative Republicans.

Unlike President George W. Bush, McCain offered a parallel to Theodore Roosevelt, who served as Colonel of the "Rough Riders" regiment he helped form, and was a hero in the Spanish American War in the late 1890s. Earlier Roosevelt, a native of New York, had spent 2 years in ranching out west in Dakota Territory following the death of his first wife.

Theodore Roosevelt was elected vice president when William McKinley was elected president in 1900. Roosevelt, Governor of New York, had been supported for the Republican vice presidential nomination by conservative New York Republicans, who considered him too liberal and wanted him out of the state. Roosevelt became president in 1901, following the assassination of President McKinley.

Theodore Roosevelt won the presidential election in 1904 and continued as president until 1909. In 1908 Roosevelt supported the nomination and election for president of William Howard Taft. Taft had served under Roosevelt as High Commissioner of the Philippines and organized United States Territorial Government there, after American defeat during Roosevelt's presidency of the Philippines insurrection that followed the Spanish American War. Taft then served as Roosevelt's Secretary of the Army.

Dissatisfied with Taft's presidency (1809 - 1813), Theodore Roosevelt again sought the Republican Party nomination in 1912. When he failed to gain it he formed a Progressive Party in an attempt to defeat both Taft, the Republican Party nominee, and the Democratic Party nominee (Thomas) Woodrow Wilson. Roosevelt's 1912 Progressive Party became known as the "Bull Moose" Party because he said, after being shot in an assassination attempt, that he was "strong as a bull moose".

In 2008 John McCain, the Republican Party presidential nominee, made a most surprising selection for his vice presidential nominee. He chose Sarah Palin, Governor of Alaska (a native of Idaho), said to be "able to kill and dress a bull moose in the field".

THE 2008 DEMOCRATIC PARTY NOMINEE

The Democratic Party nominee for the 2008 presidential election was one-term US Senator Barack Obama of Illinois (a native of Hawaii). Obama, the son of a white mother and an African father from Kenya, was born in Hawaii. From age 6 to 12 he lived in Indonesia with his mother and an Indonesian stepfather. Then he lived in Hawaii with his maternal grandparents until at age 18 he came to the US mainland to enter college. His maternal grandparents and his mother had lived in Wichita, KS and Seattle, WA before moving to Hawaii.

Following college in California and graduation from Columbia University in New York City, Barack Obama worked as a community organizer in the African-American community in Chicago. Then he completed law school at Harvard University, and returned to Chicago to continue community organizing, before practicing law and teaching US constitutional law. After entering politics and rising to first term US Senator from Illinois, Obama sought and gained the Democratic Party nomination in 2008.

Obama won the Democratic Party nomination following the elimination of other candidates and a grueling competition with Senator Hillary Clinton of New York, wife of former president William Jefferson Clinton. It had been anticipated earlier that Hillary Clinton would easily win the nomination. The competition between Hillary Clinton, a strong woman candidate, and Barack Obama, an African-American man, was history- making.

Many expected Barack Obama to select Hillary Clinton to be the

Democratic Party vice presidential nominee. The possible selection of Hillary Clinton for vice president offered a parallel to George Clinton, who was vice president under Thomas Jefferson in 1805 - 1809 and James Madison 1809 - 1812. However, Obama selected Joseph Biden of Delaware (a native of Pennsylvania) who had served in the US Senate for 32 years. Later, President Obama named Hillary Clinton Secretary of State.

THE 2008 ELECTION RESULT

The 2008 presidential election witnessed the defeat of the Republican Party nominee John McCain by Barack Obama, the Democratic Party nominee. Obama was inaugurated as the 44th president in January 2009. Where does Obama's presidency fit in the century long cycles of the United States presidency?

Two centuries ago in 1808 Democratic Republican James Madison, perhaps best known for his role in the composition and adoption of the US Constitution, won the presidential election. He defeated Federalist candidate Charles Cotesworth Pinkney, who lost for a second time. Madison was re-elected again in 1812, defeating DeWitt Clinton, nominated by a separate Democratic Republican caucus but supported by the Federalists.

In 1908, a century after Madison's 1808 election as president, Republican William Howard Taft, won the presidential election by defeating Democrat William Jennings Bryan, who lost for a third time. Taft was not re-elected to the presidency in 1912, but later became Chief Justice of the US Supreme Court.

A possible parallel between Obama's 2008 election, and either that of Madison in 1808 and Taft in 1908, is strong interest in the United States Constitution. However, earlier discussions of George W. Bush's presidency revealed an offset of 4 years in the presidential cycle. Consequently, it should be noted that parallels between John McCain, and the comment that Sarah Palin of Alaska could "kill and dress a bull moose" in the field, could point to Theodore Roosevelt and his "Bull Moose" Party in the 1912 election.

In 1912 (Thomas) Woodrow Wilson won the presidency by defeating both Theodore Roosevelt and Taft. Wilson, a native of the South, and a professor at Princeton University, can be considered a reformer as

President of Princeton, Governor of New Jersey, and US President (1913 - 1921). Woodrow Wilson was a liberal in all except his attitude toward Blacks.

Barack Obama, elected president in 2008 might be considered a cyclical parallel either to Woodrow Wilson elected in 1912 or to James Madison, elected in 1808 and re-elected in 1812. However, Obama might be considered a cyclical parallel to William Howard Taft elected in 1908 but not re-elected in 1912.

THE OBAMA PRESIDENCY

Inaugurated as the 44th president (2009 -), Barack Obama was confronted by a major economic crisis in the United States and in other countries throughout the world. It is increasingly evident that this recession (a parallel to one in 1907) is the worst since the Great Depression, which began with the stock market crash in 1929 and continued until WWII. It is a result of the influence of major financial and business interests, which gained increased political strength beginning with the Reagan administration in the 1980s. The government has failed to adequately regulate the financial system, allowing market speculation and excessive lending, bank asset manipulation, and excessive growth in the economy and consumer spending.

Like President George W. Bush before him President Obama supported large infusions of federal money to save major Wall Street financial institutions and stimulate bank lending, to increase business investment, and employment.

To ease employment financial assistance was given also to the Big Three automobile manufacturers. Funds have been made available to state and local governments for infrastructure improvement.

President Obama has emphasized the need for clean energy production and efforts to maintain the environment and curb climate change. He has gained passage of a national health plan for the United States, but the Republicans are supporting attempts by Republican dominated state governments to gain judicial elimination of the health plan requirement that all persons purchase health insurance.

To combat the continuing economic crisis President Obama proposes steps to stimulate needed business investment and increase employment, while seeking to balance the federal budget over the long term. He proposed an end to the President George W. Bush - initiated tax cuts for those with incomes of $250,000 or more plus elimination of various loopholes in the tax laws. The Republicans in Congress adamantly opposed any tax increases on higher incomes, asserting that the Obama administration and the Democrats in Congress were engaging in "class warfare". The Republicans want to reduce government, particularly the entitlement programs of Medicare and Social Security.

The United States faces the continued threat of terrorist violence by Al-Qaeda. Continued conflict in Iraq, the re-emergence of the Taliban in Afghanistan and political instability in Pakistan along the border Afghanistan are major problems. Obama is seeking a gradual withdrawal of the United States from the costly military campaigns in Iraq and Afghanistan while leaving stable democratic government in each country.

There is continued conflict in Somalia, accompanied by piracy off the coast. Sudan has been divided into two nation states but conflict is continuing between Muslim populations and the Christian/Animist populations in other North Central African areas.

Support of the recent "Arab Spring" rebellions in Tunisia, Libya, Egypt, Yemen and Syria could improve the reputation of the United States in Europe and the Middle The people are seeking the end of autocratic rule and the initiation of democratic freedoms.

The United States faces the sixty-year long conflict between Israel and Palestine. An entirely equitable solution to the conflict providing natural resources for two separate homelands and two capitols in Jerusalem is essential to any long-tern peace between Western nations and the Moslem world.

With regard to possible major conflicts, it should be noted that during James Madison's presidency the United States was at war with Great Britain (1812 - 1815), and during Woodrow Wilson's presidency the United States was in WW I (1917- 1918). Those wars plus current war problems suggest the need, not only for Obama's presidency but presidencies that follow, to seek to advance peace, education, health, and democratic governments throughout the world.

LOOKING AHEAD

This examination of the 44 presidencies of the United States, since the US Constitution was adopted in 1787, suggests that the presidencies have been under the influence of cyclical forces. More detailed examination of the United States presidencies by historians could reveal additional support for that conclusion.

Historians who examine past eras of time and significant events might gain further knowledge about cyclical influences. They might then be able to express concern about possible future issues arising from cyclical influences.

Some time ago a historian noted the possibility of cycles in war, and this review of the United States presidencies offers support for that conclusion. Humans possess initiative and wars can be avoided by enhanced diplomatic efforts to seek peaceful solutions to disagreements emanating from national security concerns or economic and social conflicts. Equitably negotiated diplomatic compromises and armament reductions can be most helpful in such situations.

Need exists for the United States and other nations to emphasize the international cooperation first envisioned by Woodrow Wilson's League of Nations at the end of World War I, and broadened in the United Nations, founded at the end of World War II. Greater respect for and support for international law, and the international system of justice, would be valuable for citizens of all nations.

The need for increased international cooperation between nations has grown with the advances in transportation and communication, and the emphasis placed on free trade since World War II. Unfortunately, free trade has not been as beneficial as it might have been to the poor nations of the world, because major business interests in more wealthy nations have exploited lower cost labor in poorer nations in order to increase corporate profits. The possible advantages of free trade need greater emphasis, and the disadvantages which have been revealed both in poor nations and wealthy nations need correction. Needed too are greater efforts by wealthy nations to assist the advancement of education and health care in Third World countries.

The increasing strength of orthodox and fundamentalist views within major religious faiths, and accompanying intensity of ethnic conflicts between peoples around the world, present another problem. With the burgeoning growth of human population, the overuse of the Earth's limited resources and the impact of climate change, thoughtful steps to concentrate on points of agreement and emphasize common views among the major religions could be most helpful. Increased emphasis on seeking ethnic and cultural commonality among people is needed as migration and movement of people increase due to the ease of travel.

THE REVERSAL IN POLITICAL VIEWS

The following conclusion has been drawn from this review of the elections and presidents of the United States. During more than two centuries of time there has been a gradual reversal of the views of the major political factions in the United States. Those views concern the importance of the power and duties of the federal government versus those of the states.

The Federalists of the 1790s, led by Alexander Hamilton of New York, believed that a relatively strong federal government was essential to the long term unity and success of the newly independent United States and its 13 states (formerly 13 British colonies). The Democratic Republicans led by Thomas Jefferson of Virginia favored "states' rights", greater power for the individual states and less power at the federal government level.

France had rendered support during the American War for Independence. Although a slave owner, Thomas Jefferson, leader of the Democratic Republicans, was sympathetic to the French Revolution of 1789. The Federalist Party, first led by Alexander Hamilton, gradually lost strength during the era of continuing British/French conflict that followed the French Revolution of 1789. The Federalists did not support the War of 1812 - 1815 with Great Britain. Democratic Republican President James Madison had hoped to avoid the war with Great Britain, but war hawks, many of them Democratic Republicans, hoped to take control of Canada from Great Britain and pushed Madison into the war. Being weakened, the Federalists supported DeWitt Clinton, the nephew of Democratic Republican George Clinton, for the presidency in 1812. President Madison was re-elected.

The Federalist Party finally came to an end with its loss to the Democratic Republicans and James Monroe in the 1816 presidential election. However, Federalist political views persisted and gradually gained strength within the Democratic Republican Party itself. Those views surfaced and resulted in bitter intra-party conflict within the Democratic Republican Party during the presidential election of 1824. The result was the presidency of John Quincy Adams of Massachusetts.

In 1828 the supporters of a second presidential term for John Quincy Adams were defeated by Andrew Jackson. The long-standing differences on political views regarding "states' rights" grew during the first term presidency of Andrew Jackson of Tennessee. The result was major conflict in 1832 between Jackson and his vice-president John Calhoun of South Carolina, a strong supporter of "states' rights". Jackson is considered the founder of the Democratic Party which replaced the Democratic Republican Party after 1832. The conflict over "states' rights" continued to grow in the 30 years prior to the American Civil War.

The political views considered conservative continued on in Henry Clay's National Republican Party faction in the 1832 presidential election, also won by Andrew Jackson. Those views appeared again with Clay's successor Whig Party presidential candidates in 1836 and 1840.

Democrat Martin Van Buren won the presidential election in 1836 but failed to gain re-election in 1840, when Whig Party candidate William Henry Harrison was elected president. Van Buren had not supported annexation of the Republic of Texas, desired by Southern Democrats. When Harrison died in office, the vice president John Tyler, a Virginian and former Democratic Republican, who believed in "states' rights", reversed Harrison's position. The Whigs expelled Tyler from their party.

Henry Clay himself was the Whig Party presidential candidate in 1844 when Democrat James Polk was elected president. Clay lost to Polk as the result of his waffling on the question of annexing the Republic of Texas, and the new anti-slavery Liberty Party's gaining some Whig votes.

In 1848 the Whigs gained their last success. The Democratic Party candidate Lewis Cass was defeated by the Whig Party presidential candidate General Zachary Taylor. The Free Soil Party, which wanted slavery banned in annexed territories, supported former Democrat president Martin Van Buren. Although a slave owner, President Zachary Taylor opposed the expansion of slavery in western territory proposed in the Compromise of 1850. When President Taylor died in office his successor Millard Fillmore reversed Taylor's position.

In 1852 the Whig Party candidate General Winfield Scott resisted the anti-immigrant and anti-Catholic prejudice growing within the Whig Party and allied himself with the anti-slavers. Unfortunately, the Free Soilers Party candidate gained only half as many votes as former president Martin Van Buren had in 1848. The result was election of Democrat Franklin Pierce for president.

The Whigs were splintered after their loss in the 1852 presidential election. Former Whigs met as the American Party convention in 1855. The most conservative wing of the American Party was openly anti-immigrant and anti-Catholic and became known as the "Know Nothing" Party. One group of the American Party voted to support "popular sovereignty" and the admission of Kansas as a free state.

In 1856 the "Know Nothing" Party nominated former president Millard Fillmore, who had become president following Zachary Taylor's death in 1850. As president, (1850 - 1853) Fillmore had reversed the position of Taylor and supported the Compromise of 1850. One provision of that compromise required the federal government to return run-away slaves. Fillmore had also refused to join the Republican Party, which was being formed in 1854 by the Free Soilers, the Northern Democrats who opposed slavery, and Northern Whigs. A small group from the short-lived American Party called the "Conscience Whigs" joined the Republicans after 1855.

With Franklin Pierce's election in 1852, and with part of the Northern Democrats moving into the Republican Party, the Democratic Party began to split into opposing Northern and Southern factions after 1854. The Northern Democrats opposed slavery but supported decision on slavery within new states via "popular sovereignty", the position espoused by Democrat Stephan Douglas of Illinois. The Southern Democrats favored "states' rights" and slavery.

In 1856, as the Civil War neared, the Republican Party, newly formed in 1854, failed to elect John Fremont as president. He lost to Democrat James Buchanan, who was able to win with Southern backing and support from Northern voters wishing to preserve the Union. In 1860 the Republican Party was successful and their candidate Abraham

Lincoln was elected president. Eleven Southern states seceded and the Civil War began in 1861.

The two Democratic Party factions gradually reunited after the Civil War but had less strength than the Republican Party. Following the Civil War, the Republican Party begun by the Free Soilers, anti-slavery Democrats, and Northern Whigs morphed into the conservative Republican Party (self-named the Grand Old Party or GOP) as we know it today. This situation continued during the era of "Reconstruction" in the 11 Southern states which had seceded at the beginning of the Civil War.

Change came when Republican Rutherford Hayes gained the presidency following the electoral vote conflict in 1876 - 1877. During that winter the Southern Democrats gained Republican Party leaders agreement to end "Reconstruction".

The alliance of the Southern wing of the Democratic Party with the conservative Republicans, in opposition to liberal positions of the Northern wing of the Democratic Party, continued until the 1960s. Then changes sought by African-Americans finally gained strong support from both Northern Democrats and Democrat president Lyndon Johnson.

Johnson, a native of west Texas, correctly forecast that his support of African-Americans would end the dominance of the Democratic Party in the South. The result has been gradual change in party affiliation and greatly increased strength of the Republican Party in the South.

Most significant since Democrat Lyndon Johnson's presidency is the increased strength of the Republican Party's support of state governments and increased opposition to regulations by the national government. This Republican Party view grew stronger during the presidential candidacy of Barry Goldwater of Arizona in 1964, and intensified during the two term presidency of Ronald Reagan in the 1980s. Reagan's presidency came two centuries after the United States Constitution was formulated and adopted in the 1780s in response to the ineffective Articles of Confederation.

The Democratic Party, now much less strong in the South, but much more unified in viewpoint, favors more power and actions at the Federal level of government. This is a complete reversal of the view of Thomas Jefferson and the Democratic Republicans who, two centuries ago in the 1790s, vehemently supported "states' rights" and opposed the stronger Federal government supported by Alexander Hamilton and the Federalists.

Since 1980 polarity between the views of the Republican Party conservatives and the Democratic Party liberals has increased. If this polarity in political views concerning the federal government continues it could in time threaten America's representative democracy, and perhaps the Union, as the conflict over "states' rights" and slavery did in the 1800s. Therefore, members and supporters of both political parties should thoughtfully evaluate the positions of their party on key issues, and American voters should carefully consider the opinions of political candidates on all important issues before casting their ballots in primary and general elections.

DID YOU KNOW?

Of the 44 presidents five have borne the surname of an earlier president. They are John Quincy Adams the 6th president, son of John Adams the second president; Benjamin Harrison the 23rd president, grandson of William Henry Harrison the 9th president; Grover Cleveland's separate terms as the 22nd and 24th presidents; Franklin Roosevelt the 31st president, a distant cousin of Theodore Roosevelt the 26th president; and George W. Bush the 43rd president, son of George H. W. Bush the 41st president.

Defeated candidates include 1812 presidential candidate DeWitt Clinton, nephew former Vice President George Clinton; 1920 vice-presidential candidate Franklin Roosevelt, relative of 26th president Theodore Roosevelt; 1940 presidential candidate Robert Taft, son of 27th president William Taft; and 1952 and 1956 presidential candidate Adlai Stevenson, grandson of former vice-president Adlai Stevenson.

DDC

ABOUT THE AUTHOR

Dale Cannady was born in Gering, Nebraska, on May 2, 1920. In his 92 years of life, he has witnessed many changes in the United States and the world.

From 1924 until 1932 Dale's parents farmed near the town of Morrill, Nebraska and the village of McGrew, Nebraska. He attended kindergarten in a one room rural schoolhouse. He attended elementary school in the village of McGrew. The 1920s saw the last active and lively years of American villages. That era witnessed the rapid rise of farm mechanization, the automobile, and the airplane.

In 1932, in the darkest days of the Great Depression, Dale's family was forced to leave the farm and moved into the village of McGrew. Dale's father supported the family with income from seasonal farm labor, service as village night watchman in the winter, and the New Deal's WPA. During those years villages died, and small towns in America became less vigorous and lively. The family remained in McGrew until Dale graduated from high school in a class of six in 1938.

In 1938 the family moved to Bayard, Nebraska, and continued the efforts required for survival in the Depression's gloomy years. Dale's limited employment, begun in his teens, was in seasonal labor on farms. One summer he went with friends and was a "fruit tramp" in northern Californian orchards. He was also employed for a time each autumn in the beet sugar mill in Bayard, and sporadically on New Deal National Youth Administration projects.

Dale's life in the Great Depression ended with the onset of World

War II, when he migrated to the Pacific Northwest. to gain full time employment at Boeing Airplane Co in Seattle, Washington. As a riveter on B17s and B29s Dale joined many men and women in building America's war machinery. After being drafted into the US Army he completed Air Force basic training at Shepherd Field (now Shepherd Air Force Base) in Texas and training at Counter Intelligence Corps school in Baltimore Maryland. He served in CIC in the American zone of occupation in Austria, where he met his future wife, Maria Neulinger.

Dale took advantage of the GI Bill to attend and graduate cum laude from the University of Washington in Seattle in 1950 at the age of 30, and was inducted into Phi Beta Kappa. His career in city planning began in Seattle and included 15 years as Assistant Planning Director in Portland, Oregon.

During a 63 year marriage Dale and his wife, Mitzi, have been blessed with three wonderful children, nine grandchildren, and six great grandchildren.